$0 to RICH

The Everyday Woman's Guide to Getting Wealthy

Tracey Edwards

Wrightbooks

First published 2008 by Wrightbooks
an imprint of John Wiley & Sons Australia, Ltd
42 McDougall Street, Milton Qld 4064

Office also in Melbourne

Typeset in Warnock Pro 11.5/15.5 pt

Reprinted 2008

National Library of Australia Cataloguing-in-Publication data:

Author:	Edwards, Tracey.
Title:	$0 to rich : the everyday woman's guide to getting wealthy.
Publisher	Camberwell, Vic. : John Wiley & Sons Australia, 2008.
ISBN:	9780731407330 (pbk.).
Notes:	Includes index.
Subjects:	Women—Finance, Personal.
	Wealth.
Dewey number:	332.0240082

Cover design by Brad Maxwell
Cover image © iStockphoto/Nathalie Beauvois
Printed by McPherson's Printing Group
10 9 8 7 6 5 4 3 2

Contents

Introduction

Not long after my first book *Shopping for Shares* came out, I was interviewed by a journalist for an article about women and money. It was clear from her questions that the skew of her story would be that women were rubbish at budgeting, and couldn't go past a store without dumping the entire contents of their wallets at the cash register.

Now, I tried to put her straight—I said that I thought that women were great with money—but she persisted in trying to get me to say that we, the fairer sex, didn't have a clue about saving for a rainy day.

The interview got me thinking: are women really good with money, or was the journalist right, and we do struggle to get ahead financially? I started looking at my friends a little bit closer. Did they have no clue about money? Was Visa paying for their lavish lifestyles, instead of their high-interest-bearing accounts? How many of us girls were sticking to a budget?

I found that nearly all the women I spoke to were good at money and budgeting, and, in fact, they were more likely to be responsible for the household expenses, balancing the finances and paying the bills than their partners. They were also more likely to have a little nest egg tucked away for those emergencies that we all run into now and then. However, when it came to investing for the future, they were a conservative bunch, preferring regular bank accounts to riskier things like shares and property.

It's not that they didn't want to get more involved in investing—just that there were more pressing decisions, like how to afford the kids' school excursions, and whether or not to get the latest Mariah Carey perfume.

But it's time to get real about our futures. This 'living in the moment' attitude will almost certainly have an impact on how we'll live when we're older. Take a look at the frightening superannuation statistics in the table below.

Average Superannuation Balances 2003–04

	Average balance	
Age group	**Men**	**Women**
25 to 34	$15 800	$11 750
35 to 44	$39 100	$17 400
60 to 64	$108 400	$36 600

Source: Ross Clare, *Are Retirement Savings on Track?*, Association of Superannuation Funds of Australia (ASFA), June 2007.

At all ages, women have about half the money in their retirement accounts that men do! According to ASFA's research, over 60 per cent of women will need to go on the full pension when they retire, compared to only 40 per cent of men. Will you be able to survive on the pension? It isn't much money—around $270 a week for a single and $450 a week for a couple (at November 2007). And while the pension will have increased by the time you retire (always presuming it still exists, of course!), don't expect that it will stretch to all the little luxuries you're accustomed to.

Okay, enough of the scary stuff. I know you've heard it all before. I also know that retirement seems far away and most of us are just concerned with getting the mortgage payments made on time. But what if you could make a difference to your future? What if it was possible to become one of those women who are financially independent? Want to give it a try? What have you got to lose?

My aim with this book is to help you get rich, or at least get richer than you are right now. I can't promise I'll make you a millionaire, but if you follow the steps outlined in this book, I can at least get you a little bit closer to it. Hopefully, as we travel this journey together I can guide you towards reaching your financial goals. Think of this book as your very own financial coach on your bedside table, helping you every step of the way and holding your hand as you make savings and investment choices.

In the first section we'll try and discover what you really want out of life. Too often we get caught up in what we think we want just because it's the latest thing or everyone else has one. But once you discover what you truly want, all the other stuff seems trivial and only gets in the way. This chapter will hopefully motivate you to start a savings plan and set up a budget.

Next we'll create a really simple, no-fail budget that will give you control over your money now and in the future. You'll be able to see just where your money goes each month and start to take more control over it.

Then comes the fun part: making money! I'll help you reach $1000 by saving, then we'll learn about term deposits and head towards making $5000, and finally aim at making $10 000 using managed funds. You'll be working alongside our character Penny Saver, so you can see exactly how she does it. We'll start Penny with an ordinary average wage and zero savings — but as you'll see, where Penny ends up financially is anything but ordinary!

If you're interested in shares and property, the fourth section is just for you. I'll give you all the tips and terms you'll need to move towards that rich future through investing wisely, whether your goal is to buy your own property or have a whole investment portfolio.

In the last section, I'll cover the all-important topic of keeping your money safe once you've got some, using insurance and a will. It's not enough to just get rich; the trick is to stay rich!

Now, are you ready to get richer?

About the author

Tracey Edwards is a savvy writer with a passion for making money. She gave up her boring nine-to-five office job after only five short years of investing in the stock market, starting from zero savings.

Author of the best-selling book *Shopping for Shares: the everyday woman's guide to profiting from the Australian stock market*, she brings her skills as an investor to this, her second book, an easy-to-follow guide to help women fast-track their financial success.

She has an arts/journalism degree from Queensland University and currently lives in Sydney with her family.

To my mother,
who thinks she's too old to start saving.
Mum, it's never too late—
—open that savings account!

STEP 1
I wanna be 'RICH'!

There was a time about 15 years ago (when I was very young and naive) that I was in a relationship with a guy who was obsessed with being rich. Everything was about money, about controlling it, keeping it and acquiring it.

He was so obsessed about it that he even tried to control my money. He'd take my pay before I got hold of it and actually give me an allowance from my own money! We had a strict budget for grocery shopping and only bought what was on special; going shopping for clothing or other luxury items was a rarity. We lived very modestly in a small three-bedroom house, and to an outsider we would have looked like any other working-class couple.

So were we rich? No. You see, he didn't have a plan or any real idea of what 'rich' meant. He just thought that if he penny-pinched and controlled every aspect of the finances, one day he'd be wealthy.

Worse, because he didn't have a plan he was often sucked into really bad schemes that promised, but never delivered, untold riches. I remember one time he spent nearly $8000 on a computer program that was meant to tell you with a degree of accuracy which horse would win a particular race. Of course, you and I both know that was a foolish decision. Yet, even after that failed, he continued to buy into scheme after scheme.

We haven't been together for a long time, and my life has turned out infinitely richer because of it, but I sometimes wonder how different our lives would have been if we'd sat down, worked out our goals together and made a realistic plan. You see, he could have got rich if he'd wanted to—if he'd just understood the steps needed to get there.

1 Defining 'rich'

By the end of this chapter, you'll have:

- created a goal sheet listing your dreams for the future
- defined what 'rich' means to you
- committed to making changes to control your financial destiny.

Rich, adj. *having wealth or great possessions; abundantly supplied with resources, means, or funds; wealthy* <www.dictionary.com>

Nice, huh? Who wouldn't want 'great possessions' or to be 'abundantly supplied with funds'? But the definition seems a little vague. What actually are 'great possessions'? I mean, 'great possessions' would mean something completely different to a Masai warrior than to a family in country Victoria, wouldn't it? How much 'wealth' does it take to be 'rich'?

'Rich' is one of those words that means different things to different people, so defining it can be a bit of a challenge. But if you want to move forward toward a better future, it's time to think about what it means to *you*. Throughout this book I'll be guiding you and helping you to increase your knowledge (and hopefully your bank balances!), but as I can't be physically there with you, you're going to have to do some things yourself. So every so often throughout this book I'm going to ask you to do some homework. I want you to do some for me now, in fact! Don't worry, it'll be fun — lots of fun actually.

Homework

Get out a pen and some paper, preferably something pretty. A journal would be good, or some patterned letter-writing paper. It doesn't matter what you pick, as long as it's something that won't get confused with an old shopping list and get thrown out by mistake!

Now, I want you to imagine that you're already rich. You're living a rich lifestyle, living in your dream house and holidaying at the best places, without a worry about money. Let your dreams run wild and picture yourself surrounded by all the things that you want from life, both financially and emotionally. What do you see? What do you have? How does it feel?

Imagine your perfect future. Do you want to live in a huge mansion with servants at your beck and call, or would you prefer a cosy cottage by the sea? Are you surrounded by books? Family? Plasma TVs? What are you wearing? Eating? Doing? 'Rich' doesn't have to mean a Hollywood lifestyle, though it could if you like.

Now, write down all those things you'd like in your future: everything that you think you'd have if you were rich. They don't need to be in any sort of order, and you can use words or draw pictures, whatever you want. Just get down on paper what you hope your future will look like, and most importantly, be specific. Don't just write, for example, 'a fast car', or 'servants'. Do you dream of owning a convertible or a Mini? Do you want your garden professionally landscaped and maintained, or does your ideal life involve spending days pottering in the vegie patch?

Your worksheet might look something like this:

No two people's goal sheets are going to look the same, because everyone is different.

Take a closer look at your sheet. Congratulations — you've just defined 'rich' for you. It's the first step in creating a fantastic future for yourself. I bet not everything on your list can be bought, because being rich isn't just about money. Sure, there are probably things on your list that will cost you a penny or two, but I bet there are also things that won't cost much, if anything.

I know what you're thinking: 'I dream about this stuff already and I'm nowhere closer to getting it, so how on earth will writing it down get me closer to being rich?' Ah, the magic of goals. Once we make them official by writing them down, all of a sudden they become easier to achieve. I don't really know how it works (*The Secret* fans will probably swear you're manipulating the universe's energy or something); all I know is that it does seem to. If you don't believe me yet, think of it this way: you need to know your destination before you can begin the journey. Writing down your goals means the plan is in motion.

It's really empowering to know what you want from life. It means you can ignore all the little distractions that don't fit in with your plan, and just focus on what's important to you. And *that* is what will help you create a rich future.

So now that you know what you want, it's time to get it — you just need to set some goals, and after all, goals are just your dreams with deadlines added. If you're willing to take action, I promise you that your life will change.

2 Goal-setting 101

By the end of this chapter, you'll have:

- chosen a goal to start working toward
- determined whether it's really what you want or just what you *think* you want.

Long ago, before I got interested in the sharemarket, a friend I'd known since high school excitedly told me that she was buying a house. She'd saved enough money for a deposit and was putting a down payment on a lovely white three-bedroom weatherboard in a trendy Melbourne suburb. Of course, my immediate reaction was, 'How on earth did she do that?' I was definitely pleased and excited for her, but also a little bit jealous of her good fortune. How could one of my friends afford to buy a house, when I had nothing to show for my years of working? I think I'd even got into a tiny bit of credit card debt, if I remember right. I'd dreamed of buying my own home, but I never took any steps to make it happen.

That's the difference between dreaming and planning. My friend and I had the same dream: she was just a little bit smarter than I was then. She knew that if she wanted something, she needed to work out a way to get it, not just dream about it. So she made a plan to buy a house and started saving for the deposit. A few years passed and voila! She was the proud owner of a house in the suburbs.

A few years later, I started setting goals myself, and went from having nothing to buying a car and a house (in expensive Sydney!), and giving up full-time work — because part of 'being rich' to me was never having to turn up to a nine-to-five job again. I did all that in five short years, because I had a plan. I also had a plan to write a best-selling book — that's how my first book *Shopping for Shares* came about.

Is it really that simple? You just start planning and working on your goals, handle your money responsibly and end up fulfilling your dreams? I think so. I don't believe that anyone gets rich by accident or luck (unless they were born into a wealthy family, and even then, there's no guarantee), but that it has everything to do with planning well. It's not like you wake up one day and say, 'Oh cool, I got rich today'. Even lottery-winners need a plan to deal with the money they win — how many do you hear about that have lost the lot within three or four years? It takes careful planning and some good sense to get and stay rich. That's not to say it's not fun — it is. What could be more fun than seeing your dreams start to come true? But it takes commitment.

The difference between my life now and my life 10 years ago (apart from a few kilos on my thighs—I really need to make a new plan for that!) is that before I knew better I just let life happen to me. If some money came my way, great, but I certainly didn't go out of my way to achieve financial freedom. Like a lot of people, I just went with the flow. The trouble with that is you might not like where you're flowing. If you plan for nothing, you'll probably achieve nothing.

What you do with your money now will determine if you have any in the future: you need to make a plan about which direction you're going to take to reach your goals. Look at it this way: at worst, you'll still end up much further ahead than you are now. So what have you got to lose?

Goal-setting is pretty much the same whether your goal is to bake a cake, take a holiday or save for a house deposit. When you break it down, there are four main components to setting your goals (in no particular order):

1 Work out your final destination, what you want to achieve—your goals

You did most of the work for this step in the last chapter, by writing down everything you'd like to achieve in the future. The dreaming part of goal-setting is always the most fun, because it doesn't matter if you think it's realistic or not. You never know what you'll be able to achieve if you don't try—who knew I'd be the published author of two great books about achieving financial success?

As I said in the last chapter, it's important to be specific: be clear about what you want and how much it'll cost (more on this in a moment), as this will make it easier to work out how long it'll take you to reach your goals.

2 Determine where you're starting from

You need to know your financial position before you can decide on the steps needed to reach your goals. I've assumed in this book that you're starting from zero, but you could be anywhere from deep in credit card debt to sitting on some pretty nice savings. Everyone's starting line is different. You'll get to determine where you're starting from soon, in chapter 3, where we'll have a look at your starting position — your X spot, as I like to call it.

3 Set a time frame for when you'd like to achieve your goals

Setting an achieve-by date makes a goal real and spurs you to act — a deadline makes it seem urgent that you get started. Of course, you'll need to make sure that the time line is realistic. There's no point planning to buy an eight-bedroom mansion by the end of the year unless you have some pretty serious cash behind you already!

4 Write down what you need to do to achieve your goals, in small, manageable steps

This is probably the most important step and the one that will get you the most excited, since you'll see your goals change from dreams to things you can achieve. There are two ways of breaking a goal into steps: you can either set time goals (for example, 'By April I want to have saved $2000'), or set out action steps (say, to open a savings account, then to set up a regular deposit into that account from your salary).

Anyone who's ever pushed a car will tell you that the hardest part is getting it moving, and that after that it takes far less effort. That's a little what goals are like. Starting is the hardest part, but once you take action you'll move quickly towards your aims, and your subconscious mind will start to believe that you can and will achieve them.

Now, let's start planning: pick one thing off your list. That's the first thing you'll work towards throughout this book, the first thing that will make your rich future a reality.

To help you along, let me introduce you to someone who'll be saving and planning throughout this book right alongside you. Her name is Penny Saver, and she's just like you (apart from not being a real person and all). She has a regular job, is interested in fashion and likes going to the movies. Currently, she has no savings and no debt, and dreams of buying a beautiful little beach house:

Penny Saver

Current savings — $0
Current debt — $0
Yearly salary — $60 619
Fortnightly take-home pay — $1803.50

How much money will your goal cost?

Some goals only take a small amount of money; for others, you'll need to save over many years. If your goal is to pay off your credit card debt of $5000, for example, it's likely to be achievable within a year — maybe even sooner depending on your income. Then there are goals that you can't price accurately, because how much they cost is likely to change in the future. The easiest way to deal with this is to work out how much your goal would cost today, work towards that figure and adjust the goal amount along the way.

Whichever category the goal you've chosen falls into, costing it will force you to get specific. In Penny Saver's case, she wants to buy a beach house. What would it cost her today? To know that, she first needs to know what type of beach house she wants and where.

Say that Penny has decided that she'd like a small house with three bedrooms on the northern beaches of Sydney. A quick look on some online housing sites tells her that the average price for a beach house in that area is around $800 000. If she were to buy it now, she'd need at least $80 000 for a deposit, and a really generous bank manager willing to give her a loan for the rest. She'd also need enough money to cover the loan repayments: around $4600 per month. Right now she can't afford it, but she might be able to in the future if she does some serious saving and investing.

So, for your next assignment I want you to write down how much the goal you've chosen costs today, so that you have an idea of what you are shooting for.

Homework

How much money will achieving your goal cost today? ....

Can you afford it now? (circle one)
Yes *No*

When do you want to achieve it by?

Different goals take different amounts of time to achieve, and as I've mentioned, it's important to be realistic about what you can do within the time frame you've set.

Penny's goal is quite hefty financially, and it'll take her a long time to save up the deposit. On her current income, she believes that she could comfortably save $300 a week. That's around a third of her take-home pay (we'll discuss budgets a bit more in the next chapter), and means that she'll be able to save up the $80 000 deposit within about five years. Is five years too long for Penny to wait to get to her goal? I don't think so: in fact, I think for buying your dream house it's a relatively short time! And saving $300 a week sounds much more achievable than saving $80 000, doesn't it? The plan is starting to take shape.

You'll notice that I haven't added in any of the interest or investment income that Penny might receive during this time. This is because if you are saving up for a goal whose price is likely to increase, like a beach house's would, the interest can help you reach this higher price without you having to change your savings pattern.

In Penny's case, if the account she puts her savings in pays an annual interest rate of 6.15 per cent (which is what most good savings accounts are at the time of writing), she could earn an extra $14 000 in interest over the five years, leaving her with over $94 000 for a down payment instead of $80 000. That extra $14 000 might be what clinches the deposit for her dream home.

What if I don't reach my goal by the deadline?

If the $94 000 that Penny has saved by the end of the five years isn't enough because the house prices in the area have gone through the roof, then she has two options. She can either save for a further few years, or if she wants to purchase right now, choose to look for something less expensive. Either way, she's still in a far better financial position than she would be if she hadn't saved.

What if I reach my goal early?

That's fantastic if you do, because it means you can move onto your next goal sooner. Pretty soon you'll have everything you dreamed of! But first things first: here's your next bit of homework.

Homework

When do you want to achieve your goal by? Choose a specific date, not just the end of the year: ..July 31/16

How much will you need to save?
Per year:..4,000..
Per pay*: $1666.60 or 333 perweek

* Breaking up your savings like this makes things easier, because you can see exactly how much you'll need to save each payday.

Stop. Is this really what you want?

I hope you aren't feeling too queasy. Putting things down on paper can either make you ecstatic that your goals are possible or depressed and wondering how on earth you're going to come up with the money. Don't worry too much about it: the next part of this book will help you find extra money to save, and the third section will help you to save $1000, $5000 and then $10 000 towards your goals.

Right now, I want you to have another look at your goal. Once you've made your plan and worked out if it's achievable within your time frame, take a second look and see if it's really what you want. It's easy to believe that you *must* have a house and a car, for example, without really thinking hard about it.

It could be that while you'd quite like a house, what you'd really love is a life full of travel and adventure. Is saving up a deposit for a house as important to you as it would be to someone whose dream is to settle down and start a family? Probably not. Maybe you could save up for a private jet instead — now wouldn't *that* be something to brag about! (Although with a price tag of around $60 million, it might be a little difficult to save for.)

And here's another reason I want you to have a second look at your goals: so that you don't write off your real dreams as impossible. Did you know, for instance, that you could hire a private jet for around $5000 an hour? A return trip to New Zealand would cost you approximately $25 000. Would that be worth saving a few years for? It would be even less if you invited a few friends along who paid their share (they'd need to have read this book and know how to save, though!). By thinking outside of the square, you could do it if you really wanted! It's certainly not out of the question. So take another look through your dream worksheet, and see if there's a way your more out-there dreams can be achieved.

STEP 2
Creating a budget

You're rolling your eyes, aren't you? You're probably thinking, 'Yeah, yeah, I know all this. I want to get onto the good stuff about making money'. The poor budget—it really gets a dud rap. Most people either insist that they're already following one or think they don't need one. If you're already using a budget, that's great; for the rest of you, I'm going to try and change your minds about starting one.

First up, I really don't believe that budgets should be restrictive in any way. In fact, the easier you make it to follow, the more likely you'll start working with it instead of against it. Those who've read my first book will know that I'm not a fan of the write-down-everything-you-spend method, even though I know it works well for some people. I prefer to make things as simple as possible, and I usually do that with the one-third rule, which I'll explain in more detail a bit later.

Getting real about the money you have coming in, instead of not worrying and just putting things on your credit card, will help you lay a good foundation for the future and, yes, get richer quicker.

3 The starting line

By the end of this chapter, you'll have:

- found your X spot (your starting point)
- paid off any debts
- learned to pay yourself first.

In step 1, you let your imagination run wild and dreamed a rich future for yourself. Now that you know what you want, how much it'll cost and when you want to achieve it by, it's time to start putting the steps into place to get it.

Have you ever looked at a shopping centre directory map to work out how to get to a certain store? Usually the maps have a big X to mark where you are, so that navigating your way to the shop is easier. Well, creating a plan to get rich is a little like that. In order to get where you want, you first need to figure out where you are now. You need to know your X spot. That's where budgeting comes in. Yes, I know, it's incredibly boring tracking every bit of money that comes in and out of your life. Let's keep things simple.

Incoming money

There are only a few ways to get money in this world. One is to have a rich family and inherit it—nice if you're Paris Hilton, but not so realistic for the rest of us. Another is to cash in a million-dollar lottery ticket—but I think there are far too many 'poor' lottery ticket holders to rely on this strategy. Lastly, there's the good old-fashioned way of earning it via a job, a business or even a government payment. As you may have guessed, I'll be focusing on this last avenue. (I'm pretty sure Paris won't be needing a guide to getting rich anytime soon.)

Regardless of what you earn (and really it doesn't make much difference whether you earn a little or a lot), if you're like most of us, you've probably been managing your money a bit like this:

1. Payday! Money is deposited into your account.
2. You pay any bills that are due.
3. You withdraw some money from the ATM so you have cash in your wallet until next payday. Of course, it never lasts, and you find yourself visiting the ATM a few more times.
4. You think about saving the money left over (if there is any). Perhaps you move some into a savings account; perhaps you blow it instead on a new dress or a pizza night.

Does this sound like you? Actually, if it does, that's good in a way, as we really only need to make a few tweaks to get you onto the right track. Just make a few small changes to your regular routine so you include a regular savings plan as well as your lifestyle, and you'll start your journey to becoming richer. I told you it'd be simple!

'But…' I hear you say, 'I *never* have any money left over at the end of my pay that I can save. How on earth is this going to work for me?' The answer is, it'll work fine. Most people don't have much (if any) money left until their next pay. Have you ever noticed that even when you get a payrise, after a few paydays you still have no money left over? It's one of those funny little money laws that your lifestyle expands or contracts to fit the amount of money that you make. If you make more, you spend more, even if you managed perfectly well before the payrise.

So, all of you who keep thinking that you'd be able to save if only you earned more money — you've got it the wrong way around. If only you stopped spending it all, you'd be able to save! The easy way to do this is by paying yourself first, before the bills, before anyone else. It's true: it's not how much you earn that's important, but what you do with it.

This brings us back figuring out your X spot, your starting place. The exact amount of money you bring home each payday now; the exact amount of savings you have now; the exact amount of debt (on credit cards or loans) you have.

Where's your X spot?

Finding your X spot (not to be confused with the G spot, which would be another book entirely!) is just a matter of doing a little financial homework. You'll need to know your net worth so that you can work out where you need to start. Perhaps you'll need to pay off credit cards or personal loans before you embark on your savings plan, or perhaps you're already ahead of the game and have a nice little nest egg tucked away for the future.

All you need to do on your financial map is to make a list of where you are now, so you know how to get where you want to go.

Homework

Income

What's your current take-home salary? 1600-1900

Do you receive any other regular income (rent, dividends)? If so, how much? ....

Debt

Do you have any credit card debt? If so, how much? 10,000

Do you have personal loans or car loans? yes

Do you have home or investment property loans? NO

Savings

Do you currently have any savings? How much? 2,000 - RSP/TFSA

Investments (shares or property)? What's their approximate current value? ....

After you've done this bit of homework, you'll have a good idea of what you own and owe, and you can calculate how much you're worth financially. If you do have any credit card debt or personal or car loans, I suggest that you pay them off before you think about starting a savings plan. Often the interest you're paying on these loans is extremely high, particularly on some credit cards and department-store financing plans. The quicker you pay them off, the faster you'll be on your way to Rich Town.

How to fast-track paying off your debts

If you've got credit card debt or personal or car loan debt, there's a smart way to pay them off as fast as possible. You'll notice that I don't put home loans or investment property loans in this 'must-pay-off-fast' category, though. Don't get me wrong, I still think you need to make your mortgage payments each month, but property loans are usually considered 'good debt', as the value of the property will rise over time (hopefully earning you a profit in the future), so they aren't considered as evil as loans for things that depreciate in value. Besides, if you wait to start saving until you've paid off your housing loan, it might take decades!

To pay off your 'evil' debts, you first need to make a list of all the credit cards, store cards, personal loans, car loans and so on that you have, and the interest rate that you're being charged on each of them. Put them in order from the highest interest rate to the lowest, and choose the one with the highest interest rate as your priority. This is the one I want you to pay off first. Pay just the minimum off all the other cards and loans, and put the most money you can afford on the debt with the highest interest rate. Once you've paid it off, choose the debt with the next highest interest rate and do the same thing until it's paid off. Keep going down the list until you've paid off everything.

Let's look at an example. Imagine that since the last few chapters, Penny Saver has gone on a bit of a spending spree. She now owes money on three credit cards with varying interest rates, and has a car loan that she wants to pay off quickly before she starts saving for her future. (These fake characters certainly know how to rack up debt quickly!)

As we already know, Penny takes home \$1803.50 per fortnight, which equates to \$3907.60 per month (\$1803.50 × 26 weeks ÷ 12 months). She's committed to investing \$1300 per month to pay down her debts.

From highest to lowest interest rate, her debts are:

Store credit card—balance \$1207.54 at 18.9% p.a.

Bank credit card #1—balance \$411.03 at 16.3% p.a.

Bank credit card #2—balance \$237.45 at 11.2% p.a.

Bank car loan—balance \$5610.00 at 8.1% p.a.
(We'll assume that she originally took out a loan of \$8000 over five years, bringing her monthly payments to \$162.50 per month.)

Total balance—\$7466.02

Typically, your monthly minimum payment is going to be 3 per cent of your total balance or $10, whichever is higher.

Penny commits to paying off the store credit card first, since this has the highest interest rate. Her monthly repayments go something like this:

Month 1—priority #1 is store card

	Balance	Monthly interest	Total due	Payment	Balance
Store CC	$1207.54	$19.02	$1226.56	$1115.00	$111.56
CC #1	$411.03	$5.58	$416.61	*$12.50	$404.11
CC #2	$237.45	$2.22	$239.67	*$10.00	$229.67
Car loan	$5610.00	$37.87	$5647.87	**$162.50	$5485.37
				$1300.00	*$6230.71*

* Minimum payment ** Fixed payment

In this first month Penny has $1115 to pay off her store credit card—the $1300 she committed per month less the minimum payments on her other debts. She's already nearly paid off her store credit card.

Month 2—priority #1 store card, #2 bank credit cards

	Balance	Monthly interest	Total due	Payment	Balance
Store CC	$111.56	$1.76	$113.32	$113.32 (paid off!)	—
CC #1	$404.11	$5.49	$409.60	$409.60 (paid off!)	—
CC #2	$229.67	$2.14	$231.81	$231.81 (paid off!)	—
Car loan	$5485.37	$37.03	$5522.40	$545.27	$4977.13

In this month, Penny has paid off her store credit card and both her bank credit cards. Now she'll be able to start paying off her car loan super fast.

Months 3 to 6—car loan

	Balance	Monthly interest	Total due	Payment	Balance
Month 3	$4977.13	$33.60	$5010.73	$1300.00	$3710.73
Month 4	$3710.73	$25.05	$3735.78	$1300.00	$2435.78
Month 5	$2435.78	$16.44	$2452.22	$1300.00	$1152.22
Month 6	$1152.22	$7.78	$1160.00	$1160.00	—

In just six months Penny has paid off all her debts, including her car loan, and is ready to start a savings plan. Remember: debt first, then savings. That's the formula for getting rich.

Pay yourself first

You've probably heard the phrase 'Pay yourself first' bandied around a lot by the financial gurus. It's quite a simple rule, really. As soon as you get your pay (or even before you lay your hands on it, if you can set up automatic debits), you take out some money and put it in a savings or investment account. Don't think about your other expenses for the moment: your future is much more important than any electricity bill, so you should get top priority. Remember that earlier in this chapter I listed the order most people do things in? Well, here's the revised order that will help you get rich:

1. Payday! Money is deposited into your account.
2. You immediately pay yourself by transferring money into your savings account.
3. You pay any bills that are due.
4. You withdraw money from the ATM so you have some cash in your wallet. You can do this as many times as you need to, as long as you aren't paying extra in ATM fees.
5. Blow any money left over on whatever you like. You've already put your savings aside, so there's no need to feel guilty about spending whatever's left.

So how much should you pay yourself? I guess that depends on how fast you want to reach your financial goals. Generally, advisers recommend somewhere between 10 per cent and 30 per cent of your take-home pay (your gross income less tax). In my first book, I was adamant that you save a third of your pay, but the cost of living is rising fast, so it's not always feasible now. When you're starting out, too, going from no savings straight to 33 per cent can be difficult.

A good goal would be to start with 10 per cent of your income and gradually increase that to 30 per cent over the course of a few years. Let's look at some examples.

Case study

Samantha's take-home pay is $1620 per fortnight. She decides to save 10 per cent of her income for the first year, and increase that to 20 per cent in the second year and 30 per cent in the third and subsequent years. During the three years she also receives three payrises from her employer. Here's how the figures look over those three years:

- *Year 1.* Her fortnightly take-home income is $1620. She commits to saving 10 per cent of that, which is $162. This leaves her with $1458 for bills and spending.
- *Year 2.* She gets a payrise! Her fortnightly income is now $1846. Since she's increasing her savings to 20 per cent this year, she's now saving $369.20 per fortnight. That leaves her with $1476.80 for bills and spending.
- *Year 3.* Another payrise, and her fortnightly income has risen to $2168. She's now saving 30 per cent, which is $650.40 per fortnight, leaving her with $1517.60 for bills and spending.

Let's look at how much money she has at the end of the three years, based on saving 26 fortnightly payments a year:

Year 1—26 × $162.00 = $4212.00
Year 2—26 × $369.20 = $9599.20
Year 3—26 × $650.40 = $16 910.40
Total saved—$30 721.60!

She's saved over $30 000—and I haven't even taken into account the interest she would have earned on her money during that time! Let's do that now. If she'd put her savings into an account that pays 6.15 per cent interest, this is how the figures would look:

Year 1—$4212.00 + $127.07 interest = $4339.07
Year 2—$4339.07 (from year 1)
+ $9599.20 (saved)
+ $564.63 interest
= $14 497.63
Year 3—$14 497.63 (from years 1 and 2)
+ $16 910.40 (saved)
+ $1429.38 interest
= $32 827.38

That's over $2000 extra earned in interest alone!

As you can see, just by paying herself first, her savings added up incredibly fast. And since she'd learned to live on the money left over (which she was free to spend on whatever she liked without feeling guilty), each time she got a payrise, she elected to increase her savings instead of her lifestyle. She didn't even miss the extra money.

But I don't have ANY spare money to save

As I already mentioned, the most common response I get when I talk about saving is, 'I don't have any money to spare.' Every cent goes on maintaining their current lifestyle (of course it does, it's the expandable money law again): they've tried saving and it doesn't work for them. Interestingly enough, it's usually people on a fairly decent salary who say this! I'm really not sure how they'd cope if they had to survive on a small government pension, and the way they are heading that's *exactly* what they'll have to do once they retire. Most people do have superannuation, which is taken from your pay before you get it—but have you checked how much you have? Will it be enough to live on? Take another look at the scary table in the introduction. If you've taken significant amounts of time off from work to have children, in particular, your super balance probably isn't what it should be.

Even if you *really* don't have any spare money, you simply have to find some in order to save. When all's said and done, there are only two ways to do that—either earn more or spend less. Earning more is usually harder than spending less, but there are ways to do it. You could be lucky enough to ask for and receive a payrise at work; you could train for a more lucrative job or field; or you could take a part-time job on the side. Maybe you're really talented at something that can earn you some money: singing at events on the weekends; making cards and selling them at market stalls; working for a party plan company on the side. You could even sell unwanted belongings on eBay to net extra cash.

Spending less is usually a whole lot easier. And I'm not going to suggest that you take a cut lunch to work every day, unless you want to. I believe there are ways to save and keep your current lifestyle. You'll be amazed at how even a few dollars a week saved will add up, and you won't even miss it. You just need to be a little smarter and more creative.

Here are a few examples:

- If you get your hair cut every eight weeks at an average cost of $40 each time, that works out at $260 per year. If you changed that to every 10 weeks instead, it'd cost you $208, saving you $52 a year.
- If you're anything like me, you need a morning choc fix. If you always spend $5 a day on a coffee and chocolate bar for morning tea at work, you'd save $260 a year ($5 × 52 weeks), if you skipped your binge just once a week (you might even lose a few kilos as a bonus). If you also stock up on chocolate at the supermarket, where it costs half what you'd pay in a convenience store or vending machine, you'd save a bucketload! Instead of $5 per day, you might only pay $2 a day, saving you $3 × 5 days per week × 48 weeks = $720.
- Instead of buying a $4 magazine every week, buy it every fortnight: you'll save $104 a year.
- On Friday pizza night, if you skip the garlic bread and bottle of Coke and buy them cheaper at the supermarket, you can save about $6. That's around $312 a year.

- If you pay $38 to get your lawn mowed by a gardener every four weeks, push it out to every five weeks and you'll save around $100 each year.

Make just those few changes and you've already saved well over $1000 a year. If you saved that $1000 each year at 6 per cent interest you could end up with:

In 5 years—around $6000
In 10 years—around $14 000
In 20 years—around $37 000

As you can see, even small amounts of money add up. Have a think about ways that you could save money without it affecting your lifestyle. Perhaps you're a movie junkie: instead of buying popcorn and a drink at the movies, take some snacks. Maybe you love eating out: go on a picnic instead of to a restaurant once in a while. I'm sure you can come up with really inventive ways to save money that are fun and won't impact on your lifestyle much.

4 The three-step no-fail budget

By the end of this chapter, you'll have:

- worked out a budget
- determined how much of your income you'll save each month.

In the last chapter, we looked at how to calculate your net worth, or your X spot. We also tossed around some ideas on how to come up with extra money to save, either by earning more or spending less. Now we need to take it one step further and actually create a budget based on your lifestyle and situation.

I'm not a big fan of writing everything you spend down—who has time for that?—but I think it's important to have some idea of what's coming in and going out. So, you need to check what your major expenses, such as rent or mortgage and bills, come to each month. (I'm sure you already know, but it helps to make sure that what you think you pay each month matches what you actually do pay.)

I like really simple budgets that are set on autopilot. The one I've outlined below is what I recommend whether you're single or in a couple, and whether you earn a little or a lot. It follows the basic rule of three—one-third of your money for savings, one-third for bills and expenses and the last third for personal spending money. As I've already mentioned, I used to be strict about each third being exactly 33 per cent of your income: so if you earned $2100 a month, you would allocate $700 for bills/expenses, $700 for spending and $700 for saving. But life is getting more and more expensive—petrol costs keep rising, food costs are increasing and housing prices are at an all-time high—so I've loosened up a bit on that rule. I still think that it's the goal you should work towards, but starting with just 10 per cent for saving is fine.

Remember the pay-yourself-first system from the last chapter? That simple method is the basis of your basic three-step budget:

1 Pay yourself first. Start with 10 per cent and see if you can raise it to 30 per cent over the next three years.

2 Pay the bills.

3 Feel free to spend the rest.

It works for any situation.

The three-step budget for couples

If you're in a relationship and you and your partner both work, it's much easier to reach your savings goals than if you were single. And even if only one of you is working, the non-working partner can provide a lot of motivation to reach your goals sooner! You're also accountable for what you spend, since you're both contributing to the budget, whether that's with money or with cheerleading and support.

Relationships Australia lists money as one of top three reasons that couples fight. I really think this is because one person (usually the one who earns the most) tries to dictate how the money is used. A power struggle ensues, the relationship is no longer equal, and as a result, bitterness and resentment can begin. Don't let this happen to you. Make sure that you both have an equal say in money decisions. Just because one person earns more doesn't mean they should have more control over how to spend the cash.

I also firmly believe that each partner should have their own discretionary money to spend on whatever they want. That way, if you want to buy a chocolate bar and a few magazines or blow all of your spending money on a new handbag, it's completely up to you. You don't want to have to report every cent that you spend.

So what's the best way to achieve all this financial harmony and still have some spending money? I think it's to pool your income in a joint account, so it becomes the 'household' money rather than your money or your partner's money, and also to have your own accounts for spending money. When money comes in, it goes straight into the joint account. After that:

1 Pay yourselves, and put money into a savings or investment account. Start with 10 per cent and try to increase this to 30 per cent.

2 Pay any bills that are due.

3 Split the remainder equally and put it in your respective personal accounts as spending money.

Let's look at how this would work in practice.

Case study—Belinda and Kevin

Belinda's monthly take-home pay—$3900
Kevin's monthly take-home pay—$4680
Combined household income—$8580

First, Belinda and Kevin pay $1716 into their savings, which is 20 per cent of their household income. Next, they pay the bills, which in their case add up to $3120. And last, what's left over ($3744) is split equally between them, so they each have $1872 a month to do what they like with.

By saving $1716 every month into an account paying 6.15 per cent interest, they can expect the account balance to look as follows over the years:

	Amount saved	Interest earned	Balance
5 years	$102 960.00	$17 228.04	$120 188.04
10 years	$205 920.00	$77 597.97	$283 517.97
15 years	$308 880.00	$196 595.71	$505 475.71
23 years	$473 616.00	$564 218.43	$1 037 834.43

As you can see from the table, at a certain point they start to earn more in interest than they're putting in!

In just 23 years they'll have over a million dollars—and they didn't even feel like they were denying themselves. And 23 years isn't really that long a time to make a million dollars in; some people buy lottery tickets for longer than that just hoping to win that kind of money!

The three-step budget for families

I know what you're going to say next. 'That's all well and good if both couples work for their entire lives, but what happens if Belinda falls pregnant and they have to live on one salary?' Okay then, let's see. Let's say that after five years, Belinda and Kevin decide to have children. At the end of the first five years, they have the same amount saved, since they were both still working:

	Amount saved	Interest earned	Balance
5 years	$102 960.00	$17 228.04	$120 188.04

But for the next five years, Belinda stays home to look after the babies, which means they only have Kevin's salary to live on. And because money will be tight, they decide to lower the amount they pay themselves first to just 10 per cent for the five years that Belinda is at home.

That means they'll be living on Kevin's salary of $4680 each month. Their savings drop to $468 each month, but their expenses remain the same at $3120. That leaves just $1092 each month to spend (or $546 each).

Yes, they have substantially less to spend on themselves (or on the kids — let's be realistic, new parents never spend on themselves!). However, on the plus side, they'll be eligible for the government's family allowance during this time.

Okay. So at the end of the five years of saving just $468 a month, they'll have:

	Amount saved	Interest earned	Balance
10 years	$131 040.00	$65 085.36	$196 125.36

Now Belinda goes back to work, which means their salaries return to what they were before she took the five-year break. Their combined household income is $8580 again (Belinda's salary of $3900 and Kevin's salary of $4680), and they increase the amount they pay themselves back up to 20 per cent ($1716). Both have $1872 to spend each month, as before. After the next five years, their savings look like this:

	Amount saved	Interest earned	Balance
15 years	$234 000.00	$152 653.10	$386 653.10
23 years	$398 736.00	$444 998.03	$843 7347.03
25 years	$439 920.00	$547 651.01	$997 671.01

It took them two extra years (and maybe one or two extra months) to get to a million, but considering Belinda had five years out of the workforce and they dramatically dropped their savings during that time, two years isn't much!

Why did it only take two years to reach the same goal? It's because during the time that they were living on one salary, the money they'd already invested was earning interest. And that interest was earning interest, and so on. Over time, compound interest works magic: that's why I'm so adamant that you put away something, no matter how small. Over time a little can become a lot!

Of course, Belinda and Kevin might have made even more. I didn't take into account that they might have got payrises during the 25 years, or that they might have invested in shares, managed funds or property for a higher return. Having a rich future is easy when things are on autopilot!

Some money terms

Compound interest—Interest that's calculated not only on the principal (the amount of money you originally invested), but also on any interest accumulated during the period. That is, the interest earns interest!

Simple interest—Interest calculated on the principal only.

The three-step budget for singles

If you're budgeting as a single person, you have the advantage of being able to choose whatever investments suit you best. You can buy what you like when you like with no guilt, and you're totally in control of your financial future. Even though you only have one salary, you can make investment decisions quickly and easily without negotiation. Amazingly enough, that means that you could end up with almost as much money as you would as part of a couple. This is because an investment's returns seem to be related to the number of people who have a say in the investment—the more people, the lower the return. It's the reason share clubs don't perform as well as individual investors. There has to be a unanimous decision on where to put the money. Not only does this mean delays in buying the investments, it also usually means that the money is put into a relatively 'safe' option, with the result being a lower return for all involved.

Don't believe me? Let's pretend that Belinda and Kevin never met and fell in love, and Belinda's a single girl.

Case study—Belinda

We already know that Belinda takes home $3900 per month. Let's say her current living expenses are $2304 per month. She decides to start conservatively, and for the first five years she saves just 10 per cent of her income ($390 a month).

At the end of five years in an account earning at 6.15 per cent, her savings look something like this:

	Amount saved	Interest earned	Balance
5 years	$23 400.00	$3926.19	$27 326.19

After this, she decides to move her money from her savings account into a managed fund. The particular managed fund she chooses has been averaging between 8 per cent and 12 per cent per annum since its inception, and she feels it's a pretty safe long-term investment. She doesn't increase the amount she's saving (remember, I'm assuming no payrises), so it's still $390 per month.

Let's say that her managed fund makes an average of 10 per cent over the next 20 years. Her balance over the years would look like this:

	Amount saved	Interest earned	Balance
10 years	$50 726.00	$24 434.17	$75 160.17
15 years	$74 126.00	$79 736.16	$153 862.16
20 years	$97 526.00	$185 825.24	$283 351.24
25 years	$120 926.00	$375 474.79	$496 400.79
32 years	$153 686.00	$890 217.81	$1 043 903.81

Sure, it took Belinda an extra seven years compared to 'Belinda-and-Kevin' to reach the million-dollar mark, but look at how little she invested of her own money! She earned nearly $900 000 in interest! I bet you won't look at $390 a month in the same way now.

The three-step budget for low-income earners

Maybe you're studying, unemployed or on a pension—there are times in everyone's life when there really just isn't that much money to spare. So, I'm going to give you a stripped-bare, absolutely-no-spare-cash solution.

I'll use the current unemployment benefit for a single with no children as a guide, which at October 2007 is $429.80 per fortnight. Just over $200 a week isn't a lot to survive on, but many people do, so it's possible. Finding money to invest out of this small amount will be hard, but I really feel you owe it to yourself to provide for your future, so try and think creatively to find ways to save 10 per cent.

Remember, most likely you won't be on this income forever. Hopefully, you'll be able to increase your income when circumstances change, whether that's through a new job, a payrise or starting a side business. You can have a richer future. However, you can still save and make a massive difference on a low income. To prove it, for this example, we'll imagine that the income of our case study, Alice, remains the bare-bones $429.80 per fortnight for 30 years.

Case study—Alice

I prefer to work on a monthly basis, so I'm going to calculate Alice's monthly income: $429.80 times 26 payments a year, divided by 12 months, is $931.23 per month. Alice is only going to save 10 per cent of her allowance, which means $93.10 per month goes into a high-interest savings account. Here's how her savings will add up over 30 years:

	Amount saved	Interest earned	Balance
5 years	$5580.00	$939.25	$6516.25
10 years	$11 160.00	$4218.24	$15 378.24
15 years	$16 740.00	$10 690.42	$27 430.42
20 years	$22 320.00	$21 501.21	$43 821.21
30 years	$33 480.00	$62 948.18	$96 428.18

Saving nearly $100 000 on a low income is pretty impressive! Now, let's see what would happen if Alice decided to move her money into a managed fund after five years, instead of keeping it in the savings account. Let's say the fund's average return is 10 per cent per annum.

	Amount saved	Interest earned	Balance
5 years	$5580.00	$938.25	$6516.25
Alice moves her money into a managed fund averaging 10% p.a.			
10 years	$11 160.00	$6791.66	$17 951.66
15 years	$16 740.00	$20 064.57	$36 804.57
20 years	$22 320.00	$45 565.60	$67 885.60
30 years	$33 480.00	$170 121.28	$203 601.28

As you can see, Alice didn't change the amount she was saving, but because she earned a few per cent more in the managed fund, she's doubled the amount she'll have at the end of 30 years.

Even low-income earners can get rich if they put their minds to it!

Can the three-step budget work if I have an irregular income?

Are you lucky enough to work for yourself, or do you have a part-time job with different hours and income levels every month? Many people in this situation think they can't save, or don't know what to save, because they don't have a set wage and their income levels can vary from month to month. Yes, the three-step budget can work for you too! It's just a matter of keeping an eye on your income for the month (or week, or whenever you have income coming in) and dividing it into three again.

Let's say that you work as a consultant and your income varies according to how much work you get. Over a two month-period you might earn the following:

Month 1—$8460
Month 2—$1233

I've deliberately chosen a huge difference between each month to show that the budget can work even on a *really* irregular income.

Now, let's say you've chosen to save 20 per cent of your income. In month 1, your budget would look like this:

Savings (20% of $8460)—$1692

The remainder ($6768) is split between living expenses and spending money:

Living expenses—$3384
Spending—$3384

As month 1's income was very high, it's probable that your living expenses will cost much less than the amount that you've allocated. Because you have such varied income, you should put this amount away in case your income in the following months is not as high. That's the case with month 2:

Savings (20% of $1233)—$246.60

The remainder ($986.40) is again split evenly between living expenses and spending money:

Living expenses—$493.20
Spending—$493.20

You didn't earn enough to cover expenses this month, but because you earned more the previous month and have some of that money put away, you'll be able to meet your living commitments easily. Not only were you able to meet your living expenses, you still managed to save 20 per cent of your income as well!

Homework

It's your turn to do the budget and work out how much you can save. Remember, the goal is to increase it to 30 per cent over time.

Your three-step no-fail budget

Year 1

Percentage to save (circle one):

10 per cent 20 per cent 30 per cent

Expenses ....

Spending money ....

Year 2

Percentage to save (circle one)

10 per cent 20 per cent 30 per cent

Expenses ....

Spending money ....

Year 3

Percentage to save (circle one):

10 per cent 20 per cent 30 per cent

Expenses ....

Spending money ....

STEP 3
Saving goals

You've done the dreaming (in step 1) and the planning (step 2), so the next step is to take that leap of faith and put all of your plans into full force, steam ahead, action! Yep, that's right, in this step I'm going to guide you along to start saving for those big dreams.

First up, I'll help you save your first $1000! Some of you might already have that money socked away, but for the rest of you it'll be a great boost to your savings goals. From there, I'll help you increase your savings to $5000 and then $10 000, through some simple investing. Don't worry, I won't make you a short-term stock market investor if you aren't comfortable with that! We'll explore plenty of investing options, so you can choose the one that suits you best.

From then, you'll be fully equipped and financially savvy enough to increase your balance on your own to whatever you like. See, I told you that you could be rich too!

But first it's time to get back to basics and talk bank accounts. After all, you need somewhere to put all that money you're going to make…

5 What bank accounts do you need?

By the end of this chapter, you'll:

- know the difference between the types of bank accounts and what they're used for
- understand how interest is calculated.

One of my close girlfriends, knowing that I was somewhat adept with money, confided in me once that she'd opened five new savings accounts. Pleased with herself, she told me that each bank account was for something different:

- her 'bills' account, which was used, as you'd imagine, to pay bills
- a 'Christmas' account
- a 'home deposit' account
- a 'holiday' account
- an 'emergency' account for surprises.

While she had good intentions, I had to ask how much she was paying in bank fees. Her answer was that she didn't really know, but she was sure it couldn't be too much, because she only ever used the accounts for saving. I asked her to check, find out the accounts' interest rates, and get back to me. When she came back, she told me that each of her accounts charged $5 a month and paid nominal interest.

While $5 a month can seem like small change, with five accounts that adds up to $25 per month and $300 per year just in standard bank fees. If she were to keep all her accounts for 10 years, she will have paid a whopping $3000 to the bank. If she'd invested that $300 a year over 10 years in a no-fee, high-interest savings account instead, she'd have a nice little boost to her rich future. Here are the numbers:

	Current situation	
	Bank fees	**Balance**
Year 1	–$300	–$300
Year 2	–$300	–$600
Year 3	–$300	–$900
Year 4	–$300	–$1200
Year 5	–$300	–$1500
Year 6	–$300	–$1800
Year 7	–$300	–$2100
Year 8	–$300	–$2400
Year 9	–$300	–$2700
Year 10	–$300	–$3000

How much she could make instead			
	Annual savings*	Interest rate 6.15%**	Balance
Year 1	$300.00	$8.60	$308.60
Year 2	$300.00	$36.73	$636.73
Year 3	$300.00	$85.61	$985.61
Year 4	$300.00	$156.57	$1356.57
Year 5	$300.00	$250.99	$1750.99
Year 6	$300.00	$370.37	$2170.37
Year 7	$300.00	$516.27	$2616.27
Year 8	$300.00	$690.39	$3090.39
Year 9	$300.00	$894.50	$3594.50
Year 10	$300.00	$1130.51	$4130.51

* Based on saving $25 per month over one year
** Interest rate calculated daily and paid monthly

Now let me ask you — which would you prefer, paying $3000 to a bank in fees or investing that $3000 and getting a bonus $1130.51 in interest? Hmmm, tough decision, huh, girls? Okay, so it's an extreme example, but it does highlight a few classic mistakes that many people make when trying to save:

1 opening a regular bank account for saving money; and

2 not investigating bank fees or other charges.

So what should you (and my overzealous friend) have in terms of savings accounts? I personally think things should be kept simple, so I recommend having only two accounts:

- One account should be at your preferred bank and will be your 'transaction' account. This is the account that you probably already have, the one that your salary is paid into and that you can access at any ATM. You'll probably only earn nominal (if any) interest on this account, and it's likely that the bank will charge a monthly fee — such is the price of the 'luxury' of having quick, easy access to your money.

- The second account should be a real savings account, an account that charges no fees and gives you a high interest rate as a bonus. I'm a fan of online-only accounts, as they have all you need and are very easy to open and use (more on these later).

Let's look at the two accounts in more detail, so you can choose one of each and get started saving.

Basic transaction account

You probably already have an account at your bank that your salary goes into. It might be at one of the four big banks (ANZ, Commonwealth Bank, Westpac or NAB), or it might be with a smaller bank or credit union. That's fine; we all need a basic transaction account to pay our bills from and provide quick access to cash when we need it.

But from now on, I want you to be more aware of what you do with this account. Don't save any money in it or use it for anything other than bill paying and holding enough cash to get you by until your next income deposit. (You worked out how much cash you need as part of doing your budget in step 1.)

I also want you to do some homework on your account. Is this really the best deal you can get at the moment? At the time of writing, three of the major banks have a regular transaction account that they promote, each charging around $5 a month in bank fees. But on closer inspection, they all have other transaction accounts as well, with fees that vary based on how you use the account—depending on your usage, some will only charge you $2 or $3 a month in fees. A few extra dollars a month might not seem like much, but do you really want to be giving the banks more money than you have to? I prefer to have those few extra dollars in my pocket!

Homework

Write down every time you use the bank for one month—every time you deposit or withdraw money at an ATM, every time you log on to internet banking, every time you walk inside a bank and talk to a teller. You could even make up a little check card like the one below and tick it every time you use a service.

Month ....

ATM	□ □ □ □ □ □ □ □ □ □ □	Total ......
Phone banking	□ □ □ □ □ □ □ □ □ □ □	Total ......
Internet banking	□ □ □ □ □ □ □ □ □ □ □	Total ......
Branch transaction	□ □ □ □ □ □ □ □ □ □ □	Total ......

What this will do is help identify your pattern of usage. Usually people think they only go to the ATM once a week, but the reality is often very different. What did you come up with? Are you primarily an online banker, or do you prefer face-to-face contact with a teller?

Once you know your banking pattern, you can have a look at the different transaction accounts available to see which one fits you best — that is, which one suits your usage and has the lowest fees. You don't have to switch banks if you don't want to: just see what different accounts your bank offers and find the right one for you.

If you do want to do a thorough comparison of how your bank account stacks up against others, you can visit <www.ratecity.com.au>. The site is run by ninemsn and CANNEX, an independent Australian finance research firm, and it allows you to compare bank accounts, credit cards and home loans to see what various institutions are offering.

Ignore the interest rate and just focus on getting the lowest fees for your level of usage. It might seem smart to have one account that you both save and transact from, but I've found that this is rarely a good solution. The interest rate paid on transaction accounts is usually so minimal (if they pay interest at all!) that it isn't worth considering.

The only other thing I'd like you to think about before you change banks or institutions is where the branches and ATMs are located. The worst fee you can get slugged for is that $1.50 for using another bank's ATM. I simply hate that fee, and it makes sense to avoid it by going with a bank or credit union whose ATMs are within easy access.

Online banking

Most of us are already doing online banking, but if you aren't I recommend getting on board. It makes it really easy to pay bills via BPAY and move money around quickly. Also, most banks don't charge for online banking, so it could potentially save you money as well as time. Internet banking is also very safe. Banks spend *a lot* of money making sure their websites are secure, and usually offer a guarantee in the unlikely event that something bad does happen.

Just make sure you never give your bank details to other people online. It sounds like a no-brainer, but con artists can be very tricky, sending you fake emails pretending to be from your bank that ask for your details. Often these emails look real and use the bank's actual logo and formatting, but if you look closely, they will usually have a long, strange return address. Your bank will never ask for your details via email. Just be careful who you give your financial info to, and you should be absolutely fine.

Reading your statement

Now that your transaction account is set up (or you've compared and kept the one you already had), I'd like you to get into the habit of checking your statement each month.

I know, I'd rather mop the floors too, but you need to make sure you're on top of your account in case there are any mistakes. It's rare, but mistakes do happen, so do a quick scan to make sure that everything is correct and that every transaction on the statement is actually yours.

Checking your statements has side benefits, too. You get much more savvy about what goes in and out of your account and you're keeping tabs on your balance regularly, making it much less likely you'll overdraw your account.

Savings account

According to a 2006 Commonwealth Bank survey, more than 7 in 10 Australians are actively saving money (*Savings Sense* survey, quoted in media release 'Australians prove they have "Savings Sense"', 23 October 2006, viewed at <www.combank.com.au>). However, the majority of us (60 per cent) are still 'saving' our money in regular transaction accounts. I'm really pleased that most people are regular savers, but I'm more excited about the possibility of you now boosting your savings by opening a high-interest savings account.

This account will be used just for saving, so ideally there should be no transaction fees and a high interest rate — the higher the better! Your transaction account was for everyday banking and paying your bills; the savings account's sole purpose is to keep and grow your nest egg.

Homework

If you don't already have a high-interest savings account, you need to set one up. You can check whether your current bank offers one, or you could open an online-only account through a company like ING DIRECT or BankWest. You should be looking for a flexible account with the following features:

- a great *high* interest rate (usually variable, but fixed is fine too)
- interest calculated daily
- 24/7 online access and customer service
- no bank fees *ever*!

Check how easily money can be deposited and withdrawn, and compare the interest rates on different accounts. At the time of writing, most high-interest savings accounts were offering around 6.15 per cent.

Once you've chosen your account, you need to set up a savings plan. But first, let me take a quick detour and explain how interest works.

Interest

In basic terms, interest is the money that the bank pays you for letting it 'hold' your cash for you. Think of it sort of as a loan in reverse: if you borrow the money from a bank, you pay it interest. If the bank 'borrows' the money from you, it pays you interest. In both cases, whoever owns the money wins!

The rate is calculated as a percentage over a period of time, with most interest rates based on one year. It sounds more complicated than it actually is. Basically, if you had $1000 in an account paying 5 per cent interest, at the end of a year you would receive $50 in interest (1000 × 5 per cent = 50).

That assumes, however, that interest is calculated only once, at the end of the year. Most bank accounts these days usually calculate and pay interest much more often, and the most common high-interest accounts will calculate interest daily and pay it to you monthly.

You want your account to calculate interest daily, because then you'll make more money—not only will the bank pay you interest on the money that you deposit into the account, it will also pay you interest on the money that they gave you as well! How great is that? You'll be earning interest on your interest, and that's when your savings are going to explode!

You'll also never miss out on any interest. Think about it. If your bank calculated interest on a particular day, wouldn't it be awful if on that day you had to withdraw your money for some reason? Even though you had the cash in the account for the rest of the month, you wouldn't be credited any interest! When your interest is calculated daily, you avoid that problem.

Let's have a look at the difference. I've just said that you'd make $50 interest on the $1000 you deposited if the interest was paid yearly. Now, let's imagine that you placed that $1000 into an account that also paid 5 per cent interest, but that the interest was calculated daily. You'd have earned $51.27 in interest over a year. That extra $1.27 might not seem a lot, but over time it will make more money and really give your savings goals a boost.

6 Saving your first $1000

By the end of this chapter, you'll have:

- increased your net worth to $1000!

Now that you have a savings account, let's make some money!

The first goal I've set for you is to save $1000. If your savings account is already flush with this amount, feel free to skip ahead to the next chapter, as I'm going to assume that you're starting at zip and building up from there.

The reason I chose $1000 as a first goal is that I believe it's an attainable figure for everybody, no matter how little money trickles your way. There's no doubt some people will be able to get there quicker than others, but even if you can only save a few dollars a week, it will soon add up. (And by the way, the more time it takes you, the more the bank will help you along by giving you interest during that time.)

This first $1000 is going to have to be made the hard way — by saving, saving, saving. Remember the budget you did earlier, where you figured out how much money you were going to save based on your income and expenses? It's time to start putting the money you decided to pay yourself into your high-interest savings account.

If you worked out that you could save $100 per week, then it'll only take you 10 weeks to reach your goal! (Plus, you'll get $5 or so in interest.) Even if you can only save $10 a week, you'll still get to $1000 in a little shy of two years, and earn around $60 in interest along the way. Remember, time is going to pass by whether you save that money or not; where would you rather be financially in a year, the same place you are now, or on the road towards a richer future? Even someone on a part-time wage can make a huge difference by just committing to saving — let's look at Natalie as an example.

Case study — Natalie

Natalie is a uni student who works part-time and has never saved before. She lives paycheck to paycheck, and it's rare that she has any money left at the end of the week. Getting paid weekly is great for her cashflow, but has created bad habits: she's never organised her finances or set a budget.

She still lives at home with her parents, so her expenses are minimal; however, she'd like to save up a deposit so she can buy a unit after she finishes university in three years' time. She's decided to start slowly: for the first year she'll put away 10 per cent of her income, the following year she'll increase it to 20 per cent, and in year three she'll increase it again to 30 per cent.

Natalie's weekly take-home pay—$301.71
Monthly total
(301.71 × 52 weeks ÷ 12 months)—$1307.41
First-year savings of 10 per cent—$130 per month

	Amount saved	Interest earned*	Balance
Month 1	$130.00	$0	$130.00
Month 2	$260.00	0.70	$260.70
Month 3	$390.00	$2.09	$392.09
Month 4	$520.00	$4.19	$524.19
Month 5	$650.00	$6.99	$656.99
Month 6	$780.00	$10.50	$790.50
Month 7	$910.00	$14.73	$924.73
Month 8	$1040.00	$19.67	$1059.67

* 6.4 per cent per annum, calculated daily and paid monthly

Natalie has reached her $1000 goal on a part-time wage in only eight months! So you can see that even on a small income it's possible to get ahead—you just need to make a commitment to yourself.

Now let's check on our girl Penny Saver and see how quickly she's reaching her goals ...

Savings goal of $1000—Penny Saver

Penny Saver's monthly take-home pay—$3906.50
Savings of 30 per cent—$1171.95

Penny's paid off the debts she racked up, and opened an online account that pays 6.4 per cent interest (calculated daily, paid monthly). She sets up an automatic debit into her savings account, and it only takes her one month to save up her first $1000.

Total after one month: $1171.95

Homework

Now it's your turn.

How much did you work out that you could save? ....

Based on that figure, how long will it take you to save up $1000? ....

I find that the best way to stick to a savings plan is to arrange for the money to be deposited into your savings account automatically as soon as you get paid. That way you never forget to pay yourself first or skip a month because Myer is having a stocktake sale, and you never miss the money! Usually it's very easy to set up automatic deposits. You can either organise it through the bank where your savings account is held (most online banks have simple instructions for doing this yourself), or you can arrange with your payroll department to have your salary split between your savings and transaction account.

Once it's set up, you can just sit back and wait for the balance to reach $1000. I promise it'll go quicker than you think! Before you know it, it'll be time to start aiming for the second goal—$5000.

7 Term deposits to $5000

By the end of this chapter, you'll have:

- increased your net worth to $5000!
- learned about term deposits.

Have you ever opened a term deposit? A term deposit is just a savings account that gives you a high interest rate over a specified time, in return for holding your money for that period. Usually you can't touch your money until the end of the term or you'll have to pay a penalty. Some people are quite nervous about term deposits for this reason, but you don't have to lock your money away for years: term deposits can be as short as one month. We'll be using relatively short terms to get our $5000, so you won't have to wait long to get your money and your interest back.

Most banks and financial institutions offer some sort of term deposit to their customers, but you'll need to shop around for a good one. As a guide, I think you should aim for at least 1 per cent more than you're getting on your savings account. Again, online banks have much higher interest rates than regular banks. At the time of writing, rates ranged from around 6.3 per cent up to 7 per cent interest, depending on the term — the longer you can put your money away, the higher the rate of interest they'll offer you.

Now, some of you may be wondering whether it's really worth the bother of locking your money away in a term deposit if you're only going to earn a few extra percentage points over your savings account. It's true that an extra 1 per cent probably won't make you rich, but every little bit helps. An extra 1 per cent on $1000 over two years will only earn you an extra $30, but would you walk past $30 lying on the ground? Neither would I. Any extra money that you don't have to work for is good as far as I'm concerned! Still, I feel that the real advantage of term deposits is that your money is safer in one than in a savings account come sale time. You can't be tempted to borrow some of your savings if they're locked away... not that you would *want* to cheat yourself of your rich future, now, would you?

I recommend you put your money away for the same amount of time it took you to save up your first $1000. If it took you three months, then get a 90-day term. If it took you two years, get a two-year term.

Deposit your money (plus the interest you earned) into the term deposit; and while it's locked away, I want you to start saving up your next $1000. You'll probably reach that goal around the time that your term deposit is ready to expire, at which point you'll have $2000 plus the interest you've earned. So, set up a new term deposit with the $2000 plus the interest, and save up another $1000. Keep doing this until you've reached your $5000 goal. You may find that you reach $5000 slightly faster this way than if you were just saving it, because of the interest you're earning.

You're probably wondering why you need to keep opening new term deposits every time you save up an extra $1000. The reason is that term deposits are pretty inflexible: just as you can't take money out whenever you want, you also can't deposit money when you want. But if you open a term deposit just for the time it takes you to save $1000, the deposit will be due to mature (finish) around the time you're ready to add that extra cash. All you need to do then is combine all your savings and reinvest it.

Let's look at our two girls, Penny and Natalie (the uni student with a part-time job), and see how they handle getting to $5000.

Case study—Penny Saver

> Current savings—$1171.95
> Amount to invest each month—$1171.00
> (rounded down to keep it as whole numbers)

She saved her first $1171 in one month, so we're going to count that as month 1.

Month 2

Penny's deposits her $1171 into a one-month term deposit paying 6.5 per cent per annum (p.a.) interest. During this time, she also saves another $1171.

Interest on her term deposit—$6.00
Balance at the end of the month—$2348.00

Month 3

Penny deposits her $2348 into another one-month term deposit paying 6.5 per cent p.a. interest. During this time, she also saves up another $1171.

Interest on her term deposit—$13.00
Balance at the end of the month—$3532.00

Month 4

Penny deposits her $3532 into a one-month term deposit paying 6.5 per cent p.a. interest. During this time, she also saves up another $1171.

Interest on her term deposit—$19.00
Balance at the end of the month—$4722.00

Month 5

Penny deposits her $4722 into a one-month term deposit paying 6.5 per cent p.a. interest. During this time, she also saves up another $1171.

Interest on her term deposit—$26.00
Balance at the end of the month — $5919.00

Penny now has over $5000, and it only took her five months. During that time, she earned $64 in free money (interest). I love interest!

Of course, it's going to take our university student Natalie a little longer than Penny. Let's crunch her numbers now.

Case study—Natalie

Current savings—$1060.98
Amount to invest each month—$130.00
(This will rise to 20 per cent or $261 in year 2 and 30 per cent or $392 in year 3; I've rounded off the savings to whole numbers again just to make things simple.)

She saved her first $1060 in eight months.

Year 1—months 9 to 12

Natalie deposits her $1060 into a six-month term deposit paying 7 per cent p.a. interest. During this time, she also saves up another $520 and earns $4 interest (as you can see in the table below).

Interest on her term deposit—$0 (it hasn't yet matured)
Balance at the end of the year—$1584

	Amount saved	Interest earned	Balance
Month 9	$130.00	$0	$130.00
Month 10	$260.00	0.70	$260.70
Month 11	$390.00	$2.09	$392.09
Month 12	$520.00	$4.19	$524.19

Year 2—months 1 to 12

Natalie sticks to her promise and starts saving 20 per cent of her income—$261 a month.

	Amount saved	Interest earned	Balance
Balance from last month	$520.00	$4.19	$524.19
Month 1	$781.00	$6.97	$787.97
Month 2	$1042.00	$12.58	$1054.58

At the end of month 2, the term deposit of $1060 matures and pays $38 in interest.

Interest on her term deposit—$38

Balance at the end of year 2, month 2—$2152

She puts all that money into a new term deposit and keeps saving into her high-interest account, as follows:

	Amount saved	Interest earned	Balance
Month 3	$261.00	$0	$261.00
Month 4	$522.00	$1.40	$523.40
Month 5	$783.00	$4.19	$787.19
Month 6	$1044.00	$8.40	$1052.40
Month 7	$1305.00	$14.03	$1319.03
Month 8	$1566.00	$21.08	$1587.08

At the end of month 8, the term deposit of $2152 matures and pays $76 in interest.

Interest on her term deposit—$76

Balance at the end of year 2, month 8—$3815

Again, the whole $3815 goes into a new term deposit.

	Amount saved	Interest earned	Balance
Month 9	$261.00	$0	$261.00
Month 10	$522.00	$1.40	$523.40
Month 11	$783.00	$4.19	$787.19
Month 12	$1044.00	$8.40	$1052.40

At the end of year 2, month 12:

Savings account—$1052
Term deposit—$3815 (will mature in two months)
Total net worth—$4867

Year 3—months 1 to 2

Natalie increases the amount she is saving yet again, to 30 per cent of her income. This means she's now saving $392 per month.

	Amount saved	Interest earned	Balance
Balance from last month	$1044.00	$8.40	$1052.40
Month 1	$1436.00	$13.29	$1449.92
Month 2	$1828.00	$23.14	$1851.14

At the end of month 2, the term deposit of $3815 matures and pays $135 in interest.

Savings account—$1851
Term deposit—$3950
Total net worth—$5801

In just over two years, our student has surpassed her $5000 goal. Now, since Natalie is due to finish uni at the end of this year, she isn't going to invest the $5000 into a managed fund, which we'll discuss in chapter 8, she's just going to keep using term deposits until her three years is up.

	Amount saved	Interest earned	Balance
Month 3	$392.00	0	$392
Month 4	$784.00	$2.10	$786.10
Month 5	$1176.00	$6.30	$1182.30
Month 6	$1568.00	$12.62	$1580.62
Month 7	$1960.00	$21.07	$1981.07
Month 8	$2352.00	$31.67	$2383.67

At the end of month 8, the term deposit of $5801 matures and pays $206 in interest.

Savings account—$2383
Term deposit—$6007
Total net worth—$8390

Nat has only a few months to go to finish uni, so she decides to put her whole savings into her savings account now, rather than reinvest in a term deposit.

	Amount saved	Interest earned	Balance
Month 9	$8782 ($8390 + $392)	$44.86	$8826.86
Month 10	$9174	$92.06	$9266.06
Month 11	$9566	$141.61	$9707.61
Month 12	$9958	$193.51	$10151.51

Just over $10 000 isn't a bad bank balance to have at the end of a three-year uni course, is it? What a great start to Nat's future, instead of finishing broke like most students do!

Remember that Natalie did this on a part-time income—like I've said before, it's not what you have, it's what you do with it that matters. If I'd only known that when I was at uni... ah well!

Homework

Shop around for a term deposit that suits your needs. You should be looking for one that takes a minimum deposit of $1000 or less (because that's how much money you're starting with), and has an interest rate at least 1 per cent higher than you're receiving from your savings account. You should also make sure there are no fees to pay.

If you've been following along and investing in term deposits yourself, guess what! You are now officially diversified—you have money in a savings account and a term-deposit account. It's true that they're both low-risk money investments, but they are investments nonetheless, and part of your growing portfolio.

Now that you have $5000, it's time to move away from the secure investments of savings accounts and term deposits and get a bit risky—you're going to start investing in the sharemarket through managed funds.

8 Managed funds to $10 000

By the end of this chapter, you'll have:

- increased your net worth to $10 000!
- learned about the benefits of investing in the stock market
- learned about managed funds.

You've been saving well and reaping the rewards of high-interest accounts and term deposits, and now you have enough money to afford to take a little more risk in order to get a higher rate of return. I'm a huge fan of the stock market for that. It's true that shares can go up and down like a roller-coaster, but if you're smart about your options and invest wisely, then statistics show that an investment in shares over the long term (10 years or more) does very well indeed. Over the last 10 years in Australia alone, the All Ords has more than doubled in value—and that takes into account both the good and bad years! It went from 2735.1 in July 1997 to 6187.5 in July 2007, as you can see from the graph below.

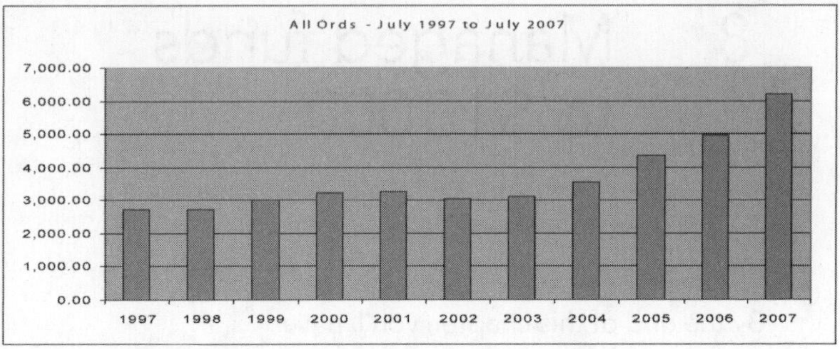

Microsoft product screenshot reprinted with permission from Microsoft Corporation.

A few sharemarket terms

All Ords—The All Ords, or the All Ordinaries Index, to give it its full name, is the benchmark index that Australia uses to track how the Australian sharemarket as a whole is doing (which is why it's the one quoted on the news each night). It tracks the share prices of around 500 of the largest companies listed on the ASX.

ASX—the Australian Securities Exchange is the market through which companies' shares are listed (along with many other investments such as commodities, futures and warrants), so that you can trade them.

The downside of shares

I'm not going to lie to you. The stories you hear on the news about sharemarket crashes are true, although they're very sensationalised. Stocks don't always go up, and companies don't always make a profit—some even collapse, like HIH and One.Tel did, and take your money with them. However, a good, diversified selection of shares can reduce that risk. Also, it's rare that shares are here one day and gone the next; they usually collapse over a period of weeks or months. So, if you're savvy, you should be able to recognise the signs and get out before too much of your money disappears.

During the devastating market crash of October 1987, the All Ords fell from around 2100 points to 1200 points, reducing the value of investors' portfolios by nearly half. Of course, they wouldn't have lost that much unless they owned parcels of all the shares in the All Ords, bought those shares the day before the crash and sold them the day after — if so, talk about unlucky! Still, it was bad news.

Historically, markets always recover from crashes. Even after the October 1987 crash, the sharemarket bounced back after seven years (yes, it was a particularly nasty fall), and if you held onto your shares until 1997 (10 years later), you'd have had a nice tidy profit to boast about again.

No-one knows when the market is going to crash next or when it's going to rise to new highs for that matter. Financial journalists seem to predict a market crash every few months, and sooner or later they're bound to be right! But even if you're unlucky enough to be involved in a crash, you'll most likely get your money back in time if you sit tight and ride it out.

The upside of shares

Even taking into account market crashes, the stock market historically makes around 10 per cent per annum — which is a lot better than the high-interest savings account and term deposits you already have working for you.

Did you know that even with a modest gain of 10 per cent per year, you'd double your money in around seven years? That means that, even if you don't keep saving, if you invest $5000 you could have nearly $10 000 in seven years — and almost $55 000 in 25 years. I bet that sounds more like the rich future I've been promising you. Here are the figures:

Compound interest of 10 per cent per annum

	Years					
	1	**2**	**5**	**7**	**10**	**25**
$5000	$5500	$6050	$8053	$9744	$12 969	$54 174

Getting your feet wet in shares

As you're still learning about the sharemarket, I'm not going to ask you to invest directly in shares just yet — there'll be plenty of time for that later. You're going to be putting your money into the sharemarket via managed funds instead. You'll still get the benefits of investing in the sharemarket, but since you only have a small amount of money to invest at this stage (the $5000 you've saved up), it makes sense to let the professionals handle things for now.

Managed funds are simply professionally managed investment portfolios that you can buy into. You purchase 'units' of the fund instead of buying shares direct. The benefit is that for a small amount of money, you can own a slice of potentially thousands of shares. It's a great way of diversifying your investments over different types of assets, companies, industries, sectors and even different countries.

Reasons to invest in a managed fund:

- *The professional management.* If you've never invested in the sharemarket and you don't know your return on equity from your debt-to-equity ratio, leave it up to the professionals for a while. The theory is that these guys (and yes, they usually are guys) do this for a living and so should know what they're doing. You can take advantage of their expertise for just a small fee for opening a fund account.

- *Diversification.* Starting with $5000 means that buying shares directly is high-risk, since you can't spread your money between very many different companies and asset classes. With managed funds, however, your money is pooled with all the other investors' money and used to buy hundreds of different companies — thus lowering the risk.

- *Low start-up costs.* You can enter many managed funds with as little as $1000.

- *Minimal paperwork.* That's what they pay the fund manager for (or rather, they pay him to make his assistants do it). All the paperwork is done, and all you have to do is sit back and wait for the statements of your net worth to roll in.

The drawbacks of a managed fund:

- *No control over investment choices.* Since you're leaving all the decisions about which shares to invest in to the fund professionals, you have no say. And even if they've done a good job in the past, things can change: the people handling the fund may well move on and the new staff might not be quite as good at picking winners.
- *Diversification means diluted profits.* Investing in hundreds of companies means that your risk is lower, but so is your profit. If one company does exceptionally well and another falls in price, the second company will pull down the profits you made on the first.
- *Fees.* Some funds can be expensive, and it's worth looking at what fees are charged. Do they charge an entry and exit fee? What about fees for depositing additional money?

Finding a managed fund to invest in is easy, but choosing one to invest in is hard. There are so many funds, each offering different investment options, it can be hard to know where to start.

What is, and how do you find, a fund manager?

A fund manager is a person or company responsible for making decisions regarding a portfolio of investments.

There are a lot of fund managers in Australia, and it can be hard to find out which one is the best. Here's a list of some of the more popular fund managers to get you started:

- AMP Capital Investors
- Asgard
- BT Financial Group
- Colonial First State
- ING
- Macquarie Financial Services Group
- Merrill Lynch
- MLC
- Perpetual.

You can usually download a fund manager's prospectus online or, if you prefer, you can call and ask them to send you a hard-copy version. I think it's a good idea to look at brochures from at least three different fund managers, so that you can compare the type of investments they offer and their performance over the last one, five and 10 years.

You can also head to <www.morningstar.com.au> or look in the finance section of your newspaper to find out which funds are good. Morningstar has a star rating system that ranges from one star up to five stars: choosing a four- or five-star fund should ensure you get a decent one. Don't choose a fund just because it has the highest return, though. As they say, past performance is no guarantee of future performance!

What to look for in a managed fund

There are a lot of things to consider when choosing a managed fund. I recommend that you look first for a stable and reliable fund management company with low fees, which has funds that have performed consistently well over the last 10 years.

Next, you need to decide how much risk you're comfortable with. Unless you're sure you'll be happy with a higher risk, for now it might be worth sticking to a 'diversified' or 'balanced' managed fund at the fund manager of your choice. These will give you good capital growth by investing in a mixture of cash, fixed interest, property and shares.

Also, take note of whether the fund charges any fees for depositing or withdrawing money. Most do charge a small fee, but the fee amount can vary widely between different fund management companies, so it's good to have a look at a few different companies to see how they compare.

What if I already have a financial planner?

If you already have a financial planner, great! Most of the hard work will be done for you, and you just need to discuss with your planner what managed funds he or she recommends, based on the level of risk you're happy with.

Buying into the fund

Once you've made your decision, it's time to send the application form and your $5000 (plus interest) to the company and get your investment up and running. You can usually apply online to make things quicker.

Now, your money is invested in a managed fund and happily growing at (hopefully) around 10 per cent per annum. I want you to keep on saving up your thousands, but now, instead of putting each $1000 into a term deposit, add it to your managed fund until you reach your new goal of $10000.

Money terms

Diversified managed fund—A diversified fund invests in a broad range of assets. Its investments usually consist of a mixture of cash, fixed interest, shares and property, and may include both Australian and global assets.

Balanced managed fund—A balanced fund is similar to a diversified fund in that it invests in a broad range of assets, but usually this allocation is balanced 50/50 between low-risk assets, like cash and fixed interest, and higher-risk growth assets, such as shares and property.

Case study—Penny Saver

Penny has decided to place her $5919 into a diversified fund, which she notes has averaged around 10.5 per cent p.a. over the last 10 years. This isn't a guarantee that it'll earn the same in the future, but the fund's earnings have been stable since its inception and she feels happy with this level of risk.

While her money is in the managed fund, she continues to save into her high-interest savings account, and every time she reaches $1000 she adds this to her managed fund. Managed funds are much more flexible than term deposits; you can add money into the fund (usually in increments of $1000 or more) anytime you like. Some smaller companies do have rules on when and how much you can deposit, and may charge a small fee for deposits and withdrawals. As mentioned earlier, it's best to check what your fund allows. Saving up $1171 per month, Penny is able to make regular deposits into her managed fund every month.

Penny's current net worth—$5919.00
Monthly savings—$1171.00

Months 6 to 9

Penny deposits her $5919 into the managed fund, and every month adds her savings. In the time that Penny is in the fund, it increases by an average 13.92 per cent a year.

	Deposits	Balance	Managed fund value*
Beginning of month			$5919
Month 6	$1171	$7090	$7159.05
Month 7	$1171	$8261	$8413.56
Month 8	$1171	$9432	$9682.71
Month 9	$1171	$10603	$10966.66

* with average 13.92 per cent p.a. increase

After just nine months, Penny has gone from zero savings to nearly $11000, and the year isn't even over yet!

By now you've probably spotted the flaw in my calculations, though—it would be very rare indeed that a managed fund earned the same amount month to month, as shares go up and down by differing amounts daily. Still, for the purposes of this example, I thought it best to keep things simple and assume that the yearly percentage was divided equally each month.

I've also not taken fees into account in this example. It's not unusual for fees to be around 1 to 4 per cent of the amount deposited, which would mean that Penny might be up for around $50 to $100. Even so, considering that she's made over $400 profit, she's still much further ahead than if she had left the money in her savings account. The fees are also a lot lower than brokerage fees on direct share investments.

As you can see, with the help of compound interest, once the ball gets rolling you can accumulate money pretty quickly. It just takes money to make money.

Homework

- If you haven't done so already, get hold of at least three different company prospectuses, and get a feel for the types of managed funds that they offer.
- Ask your financial planner (if you have one) for advice on the right managed fund for you.
- Fill in the paperwork and open your managed fund.

You should receive statements from your fund every 6 to 12 months, so you can keep an eye on how your investment is doing. Managed funds are not a short-term investment, remember, so don't worry overly if things go up and down a bit — it will even out over time and you'll come out ahead.

So now you know the basics: you've learnt how to save using a high-interest savings account, and you've invested in term deposits and a managed fund. Now it's time to take the next step, and check out investing directly in shares and property.

Oh, and congratulations on getting this far — by now if you've been doing the homework, you should be much closer to having $10 000 and a richer, wealthier future.

STEP 4
Investing in the big guns: shares and property

Ka-ching! By now you should have some serious cash saved up and earning you heaps of lovely interest. It's a good time to look beyond the simple savings account and managed fund, and start thinking about other investment options.

Today, investing in shares is very easy; you can get an online brokerage account in a few clicks of the mouse and become a stockholder in a few more clicks. Is property more your thing? Again, the internet allows you to look at hundreds of properties with the click of a button. In fact, I often wonder why anyone leaves the house these days. You can choose a property, apply for a bank loan, arrange a building inspection and even put in an offer all without leaving your desk!

Investing in property or shares will fast-track your journey to a wealthier future and get you to your goals quicker, but you do need to understand the risks involved. This section will show you not only how to invest, but also how to get an idea of the risk and return of an investment, so that you can decide whether it's right for you.

9 Getting ready to invest in shares

By the end of this chapter, you'll:

- know what to look for in a broker
- have everything you need to get started investing directly in the sharemarket.

Anyone who's read my first book will know that the sharemarket is a bit of a passion of mine. After five years of investing and saving, I was able to earn enough from my interest alone to give up working full-time, though I wasn't what you would consider 'Hollywood rich.' Of course, I could have made much more money if I had kept working and investing, but I chose lifestyle and family and feel much better (and richer) for it!

As my stock-market investing has gone on the back burner now that I have a rambunctious toddler running around my feet, I invest more over the long term so that I don't have to keep an eye on every market move. I still make a pretty decent return, but I don't have to watch the market as closely as I did when I was doing more short-term investing.

I'll explain both long-term and short-term investing later on, but let me say here that even if you're more of a short-term player, I think it's best to have some long-term companies in your portfolio as well.

Getting ready to invest in shares

Before you get started, you need to sign up with a broker so you can buy and sell shares. It's fairly simple to do. Once you've filled in the forms, you're sorted and can start choosing companies to invest in.

It's generally free to sign up, although sometimes brokers like you to set up an account with them as well and deposit some money into it—often they'll even pay you interest on this money while it's sitting in the account! It's more common these days, though, to transact through your existing bank account. I think this is easier, as you can easily deposit and withdraw funds as needed. Remember to use your regular bank transaction account and not your savings account for this.

There are three main types of brokers that you can choose from, each with different services:

- A *full-service broker* can offer advice and do your research for you. He or she will consult you, choose shares to buy based on your preferences and guide you through the investment process. The benefits are that your broker will get to know you and your investment style, and can then tailor strategies to suit you. The downside is that using a full-service broker usually costs more than the other options.

- A *discount broker* will be able to provide you with any research you request but probably won't offer you any advice or investment strategies. Discount brokers are there simply to place your buy and sell orders. Most are also online brokers, so you can choose the level of service you need.
- An *online broker* will place your buy and sell orders for you and that's it. You'll have to do your research yourself, but because of this, the brokerage fees are very low. Buying and selling shares online is currently the most popular option, as doing your own research online is pretty easy. You can place buy and sell orders over the telephone with most online brokers too, but most people prefer to transact exclusively via the internet.

If you've followed the steps in this book, you'll have more than enough money to get started investing. Around $5000 to $10 000 is a good amount to begin with, but you can use as little as $3000 if you need to. In my previous book, *Shopping for Shares*, I talked about how I started with just $1000, but I recommend you start with a little more so your money isn't eroded away by brokerage fees. Also, it's up to you, but I recommend that you keep at least half of your money in the managed funds that you already hold.

Along with cash, you also need a way to find out current share prices, especially if you're planning on doing some short-term investing. You can find out the prices online on your broker's website or the ASX website (<www.asx.com.au>), or you can subscribe to a national paper that lists the stock prices each day. You could even get really keen and watch Bloomberg on Foxtel to get the latest share prices, if you're patient enough to wait for your share price to slide across the bottom of the screen.

The only other thing you'll need to get started is a way to contact your broker: either a computer, if you're trading online, or a phone—then you can yell 'Sell 500 of BHP now!' in the middle of your high school reunion so that everyone knows how awesome (or arrogant) you are.

You don't need any special computer software when you're starting out. Yes, there are a number of professional trading programs on the market to help people with their investing and trading by choosing or researching companies, but I still haven't bought one and seem to get along just fine. Maybe I'd have an edge if I bought one of these systems; maybe not. I know a lot of people have success with them and a lot don't, so I really think it comes down to your own investment style. My biggest issue with them is the cost. Usually they're hundreds or even thousands of dollars to buy, and I can't justify spending that money when I can do the research myself.

Now that you're ready to rock and roll, let's look at investing for the long term.

10 Investing for the long term

By the end of this chapter, you'll:

- be able to do your own fundamental research
- know the rules for choosing long-term investment stocks.

As the name suggests, investing for the long term is investing in a company and holding it for the long haul — at least five years, but generally more like 10 plus. A big advantage of investing for the long term is that, on top of the capital gain, most companies will send you a nice little dividend cheque every six months as your share of the profits.

Investing long-term is simple: you do your research up-front on which companies to choose, and then sit back and keep a lazy eye on how your investments are doing every now and then. The most common way of choosing your companies is through a little fundamental analysis.

Money terms

Fundamental analysis—Valuing companies based on their financials and operations, particularly their earnings, growth, profits, debt and management. This method of analysis only takes into consideration the company itself, not what the rest of the stock market is doing.

Despite the scary-sounding name, fundamental analysis is actually pretty easy. All you have to do is compare different companies. Who has the bigger earnings? Who has the lowest debt? I'll show you exactly what to look for and where to look for it over the next few pages.

Finding long-term winners

I have a few simple rules that I use when choosing long-term stocks. These are the rules I've always used, and they've been very profitable for me. And all the information you need to follow them is listed on the companies' financial data sheet. Yep, no maths required, thank goodness! You just have to read a financial data sheet. You can access the data sheet (sometimes called a company wrap sheet) via your broker or from the company's website. It'll look something like the picture opposite.

This sheet lists everything you need in order to decide whether a stock is a good long-term option for you, including information about what the company does and its future plans. It's usually updated daily, so you can be sure you're getting the latest information.

CommSec | **GPT Group**
Code: **GPT**

Last Update: 18 December 2007

Key Measures

Value		Company	Market	Sector
		Company	Market	Sector
Earnings Model		1.25	1.99	1.14
P/E Ratio		13.56	13.03	8.56
P/B Ratio		1.14	2.12	0.95
P/E Growth Ratio		10.00	0.71	10.00
Risk				
Beta		0.85	1.09	0.96
Income				
Dividend yield		7.1%	4.0%	7.1%
Franking		–	–	–
Tax adj div yield		3.7%	3.2%	3.9%
Dividend stability		99.2%	0.0%	99.3%
Growth Rates	10yr	5yr	1yr	2yr Fcast
Sales	5.6%	9.6%	9.8%	–
Cashflow	2.8%	1.6%	35.5%	–
Earnings	7.0%	11.6%	-13.6%	-5.5%
Dividends	3.8%	6.9%	12.7%	5.0%
Book Value	4.0%	6.2%	15.8%	–

Balance Sheet ($ Mil.)	2004	2005	2006
Cash	51	94	59
Receivables	72	150	174
Investments	0	0	0
Other Current Assets	0	9	7
Total Current Assets	123	280	2,276
Investments	108	1,457	3,522
Property	8,866	7,281	5,303
Other Non Current Assets	0	1,414	901
Total Non Current Assets	8,974	10,152	9,726
Total Assets	9,097	10,432	12,002
Accounts Payable	192	248	228
Provisions	113	144	10
Other Current Liabilities	1,072	1,589	1,630
Total Current Liabilities	1,377	2,015	1,893
Borrowings	1,627	2,040	2,662
Deferred Tax	0	0	1
Other Non Current Liabilities	0	4	4
Total Non Current Liabilities	1,627	2,043	2,666
Total Liabilities	3,004	4,058	4,560
S'holder Equity (Book Value)	6,093	6,091	7,137

Liquidity	2005	2006	2007
Avge buy sell spread	0.2%	0.3%	0.4%
Annual turnover	66.8%	73.6%	106.1%
Top 20 sh/holder o/ship	79.5%	0.0%	--%

Property Portfolio Analysis

Sector	2005	2004	2003
Industrial	4.0	–	
Hotel/Resort	4.8	0.0	--
Office	18.4	38.1	16.7
Other	56.2	--	52.1
Retail	20.6	57.8	31.2

Property	
Other	52.1%
Melbourne Central	6.7%
Charlestown Square	5.7%
Penrith Plaza	5.6%
Casuarina Square	4.8%
530 Collins Street	4.5%
Macarthur Square	4.3%
Riverside Centre	4.3%
MLC Centre	4.2%
Sunshine Plaza	4.1%
Melbourne Central	3.8%

Interim Data

Earnings per share (cents)			
Period ending	1st Half	2nd Half	Full Year
2007-12-30	35.4	–	–
2006-12-30	34.5	-0.44	34.1
Dividends per share (cents)			
2007-12-30	14.3	–	–
2006-12-30	13.6	–	13.6

Most recent dividend payment dates	Interim	Final
Ex dividend date	29 October, 2007	27 February, 2007
Div pay date	23 November, 2007	28 March, 2007

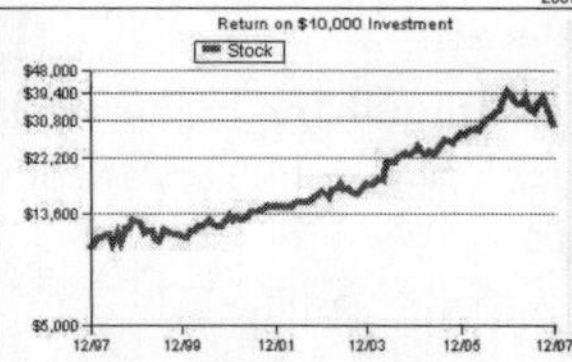

Last Price
$3.97
P/E Ratio
13.56
GICS Sector
Financials
Market Cap
$8,335m

Ann'l Shareholder Return	
1 yr	-24.5%
3 yr	8.4%
5 yr	12.9%
10 yr	11.7%

12/97	12/98	12/99	12/00	12/01	12/02	12/03	12/04	12/05	12/06	Per Share Statistics	2007E	2008E
22.9	20.9	19.0	19.3	17.2	12.9	9.50	11.4	21.3	69.3	Investment Income ($)		
0.18	0.18	0.18	0.18	0.22	0.21	0.20	0.19	0.17	0.24	Cash flow ($)		
18.5	18.3	18.7	19.3	19.7	20.4	21.6	21.3	39.4	34.1	Earnings (cents)	29.1	30.4
19.7	19.1	19.1	19.3	19.7	20.4	21.2	22.0	24.4	27.5	Dividends (cents)	28.9	30.3
–	–	–	–	–	–	–	–	–	–	Franking (%)		
-0.36	-0.18	-0.52	-0.24	-0.43	-0.40	-0.37	-0.40	-0.71	-0.14	Capital Spending		
2.45	2.51	2.51	2.58	2.59	2.60	2.73	3.02	3.02	3.50	Book value		
1,292	1,396	1,538	1,755	1,867	1,950	1,950	2,017	2,017	2,042	Shares outstanding (m)		
–	–	61.7	99.8	103	97.6	104	112	63.0	94.6	Relative PE ratio ($)		
1.11	1.21	0.99	1.07	1.09	1.14	1.10	1.24	1.36	1.59	Price/NAB ratio (%)		
22.9	26.3	-12.7	20.2	9.81	12.8	8.28	33.3	16.6	44.4	Total Return (%)		
11.4	8.48	19.3	5.03	10.1	-8.55	16.5	27.6	21.1	25.0	+/- Market (%)		
–	–	–	–	–	–	–	–	–	–	+/- Sector (%)		
331	362	424	–	515	568	606	661	690	660	Rental Income ($ million)		
22.9	20.9	19.0	19.3	17.2	12.9	9.50	11.4	21.3	69.3	Investment Income ($ million)		
10.9	8.30	185	484	123	187	42.5	20.5	136	241	Other Income ($ million)		
-87.6	-90.9	-107	-124	-126	-129	–	–	-178	-180	Property Expenses ($ million)		
0.73	0.72	0.84	0.75	0.62	0.87	3.39	3.25	1.19	1.10	Management Expense Ratio (%)		
225	249	275	317	362	386	420	426	794	692	Net Profit Before Abnormals ($ million)		
220	249	275	317	364	386	420	426	589	1,363	Net Profit ($ million)		
3,167	3,509	3,856	4,524	4,839	5,074	5,316	6,093	6,091	7,137	Shareholders Equity ($ million)		
7.11	7.08	7.14	7.01	7.49	7.61	7.91	7.00	13.0	9.69	Return on Equity (%)		
107	104	102	100	100	100	98	103	62	81	Payout Ratio (%)		

BUSINESS DESCRIPTION

General Property Trust (GPT) is Australia's largest diversified listed property trust, with total assets of $12 billion in June 2006. The Trust owns, develops and manages a portfolio of commercial office, industrial, retail and hotel properties in Australia and globally. In April 2007, GPT successfully finalized the establishment of the GPT Wholesale Shopping Centre Fund. The shopping centre fund will initially own a 1.9 billion portfolio of quality Australian retail assets.

STRATEGY ANALYSIS

GPT's strategy is to actively managing and extracting value from a core portfolio of diversified quality assets (assets with predictable cash flows, assets held for long-term ownership) and expanding through acquisitions and developments. GPT also focuses on developing a wholesale funds management platform to meet the increasing demand from domestic and international institutional investors for direct property exposure to quality real estate assets. GPT's future growth is expected to come from its retail development pipeline, recent acquisitions and setting up of the fund management platform. GPT has launched its first wholesale fund - the GPT Wholesale Office Fund.

(Last Updated: 22/10/07)

GPT Group	Tel: (02) 8239 3555 Fax: (02) 9225 9318	Chairman: Peter Joseph
ABN: ARSN 090 110 357	Web: www.gpt.com.au	MD: Nick Lyons
Level 52 , 19-29 Martin Place	Dividend Reinvestment? No	
Sydney, NSW 2000	Shareholder Discounts: Yes	

© CommSec

So, what's the first thing to look for when choosing shares for the long term?

Rule #1: choose market leaders

Market leaders are the companies listed on the Australian Securities Exchange with the biggest market capitalisation.

Money terms

Market capitalisation—The monetary value of a company. It's calculated by multiplying the number of shares available by the price of the shares.

Choosing companies with high market capitalisation means you have a better chance of getting a nice, stable company. I prefer to stick with the companies that form part of the All Ordinaries Index—it contains the 500 largest companies by market capitalisation.

If you find that 500 still seems a lot to choose from, feel free to narrow the selection down to the S&P/ASX 200 or even the S&P/ASX 100, which contain the top 200 or 100 companies based on market capitalisation. You can find a list of all the companies in the S&P/ASX 200, 100 and All Ords indexes on the website (<www.asx.com.au>) or on any financial research site.

Now, let's narrow your selection down even more.

Rule #2: choose companies with a debt-to-equity ratio of less than 75 per cent

The debt-to-equity ratio is a measure of the company's borrowings as a percentage of shareholder equity. The higher the number, the more money the company's borrowed. While some debt is normal, you want it to be below 100 per cent at least, and preferably below 75 per cent, as I've said in the rule. If the debt-to-equity ratio is higher than 100 per cent, and worst came to worst and the company went belly up, it wouldn't have any money left to pay the shareholders back, as it would owe too much to the bank.

Did you know that you could have avoided being involved in the financial collapse of HIH Insurance, One.Tel and most of the dotcom companies if you'd just stuck with this rule? All their debt-to-equity figures soared way above 75 per cent!

Just a quick note: banks and other financial institutions don't have a debt-to-equity ratio, as they're the ones lending the money, not borrowing, so this figure is irrelevant to them.

You can find a company's debt-to-equity ratio listed in the risk section on your company data sheet. Larger companies, especially those which own lots of property — like Westfield, which owns masses of shopping centres worldwide — will usually have a high debt-to-equity ratio due to the number of loans they have for the buildings. As long as the ratio is below 75 per cent, they're still usually fairly safe.

Rule #3: choose companies with a return on equity of at least 15 per cent

Return on equity (ROE) measures the amount of profit the company has made on its shareholders' behalf. Most investors use this figure to measure how a company is doing financially: usually, the higher the company's profit, the higher the ROE.

A higher return on equity means that any extra money the company makes can be invested back into the business to improve operations. It also means there's less need for the company to borrow to expand its business, so its debt-to-equity ratio should be lower.

ROE is a good indicator of where the share price is likely to go in the future. Companies with high ROE are usually pretty sound financially, so it makes sense that they'll increase in value, and thus, sooner or later, the share price will rise accordingly.

Rule #4: choose only companies that have been listed on the stock exchange for at least five years

If I'm buying a company for long-term investment, I usually ignore the new floats and initial public offerings (IPOs) that are popular with so many investors. I look for companies that have been listed on the stock exchange for at least five years, so that I can check over the history of the company's financials. A company that has been stable and earning consistent profits in the past is more likely to do so in the future.

I no longer have time to sit and watch every market fluctuation—I'm busy with other priorities—so it makes me feel much better to know I've chosen a nice, stable company that'll hopefully make lots of nice money for me.

Rule #5: choose companies with an average return of 15 per cent or more over the last five years

Not every company I invest in meets this fifth rule exactly—I'm certainly not going to write off a company because one year it returned 10 per cent instead of 15 per cent. Still, looking back over the share price return gives you some idea about the share's consistency year to year. I prefer shares that consistently produce good results; I guess I feel that if the share has performed well in the past, it might also perform well in the future. Of course, not every company that has been profitable in the past *is* going to be profitable in the future, but at least you know it isn't a fly-by-night operation.

Looking back five years or more tends to give a more realistic picture of the shareholder return than just looking at the past year. As you already know, the stock market has ups and downs, and often the share price of even a solid company will decrease just because everything else around it has fallen. One or two lower than average returns don't mean it's a bad company.

This rule works best when you combine it with the rules on return on equity and the debt-to-equity ratio. If all the figures look good, you can be more confident that you're choosing a solid company.

Rule #6: choose companies with earnings stability of at least 80 per cent

Earnings stability is the measure of the stability of earnings growth from year to year, expressed as a percentage. Consistent companies won't give you the thrills and spills of volatile company, but they can usually provide a degree of confidence that they'll perform for you year after year. I like the companies I choose to have at least 80 per cent earnings stability.

You can't choose a company based solely on this figure, however, as it only measures stability, not profitability.

A company could be losing money every year consistently and still have a high earnings stability measure—hey, at least it's consistent! But combined with good results in the rest of the fundamentals, it means the company is worth a go. In fact, I consider earnings stability to be the next most important factor after return on equity in determining a good long-term choice.

Shhh! Want to know a secret that will fast-track your research?

Every year, Martin Roth puts out a book called *Top Stocks*. The companies listed in his book usually fit most of my rules already. So, bang!—in the time it takes to hand over $30 for the book, you've knocked off two to three hours or more of research. You don't even have to read most of the book—just flip to the back to find a list of the companies rated from highest to lowest for the criteria you are after. Not bad, huh? Of course, you can still do it yourself if you want to...

PS: Martin, if you're reading this, feel free to send commission cheques my way!

What price do you pay?

So, you've narrowed down your selection to a handful of companies. Should you just go and plonk your money down on them? Not so fast. You see, to get good value for money

I like to wait until the shares are at a certain price before I buy them. I wait until the share price falls to less than 16 times the earnings per share (EPS) before I consider adding them to my portfolio.

The EPS figure is usually located near the top of the data sheet, and is generally listed in the stock-market section of your newspaper, too. It represents the total earnings of the company divided by the number of shares it has.

The reason I choose 16 times earnings is simply because the greatest value investor of all time, Warren Buffett, uses this rule. It's an amazingly simple, quick and easy way of valuing shares to see whether they are overpriced or not. Let's look at some examples.

Company	ASX Code	Current Price*	EPS	16 × EPS	Is price < 16 × EPS?
ANZ Bank	ANZ	$30.40	204.8¢	$32.77	Yes
Telstra	TLS	$4.70	26.2¢	$4.19	No
Mirvac	MGR	$5.81	57.5¢	$9.20	Yes
National Aust Bank	NAB	$43.50	251.0¢	$40.16	No
Newcrest Mining	NCM	$33.46	55.2¢	$8.83	No

* Company prices as at 1 November 2007

In the above table, two companies, ANZ and Mirvac, are trading at a price that is less than 16 time EPS. ANZ's earnings per share is 204.8¢ (or $2.048), and Mirvac's earnings per share is 57.5¢ ($0.575). As you can see, the rest of the shares that are listed, while they may all be good companies, are trading at more than 16 times their EPS figures. In fact, one company looks quite overpriced — Newcrest Mining is trading at more than four times what we'd be prepared to pay for it. Now I'm not saying that it isn't worth that much, but I wouldn't be buying it just yet, in case it's due for a correction (that is, a fall).

Assuming that the rest of their financials were stable, we'd be buying ANZ and/or Mirvac based on these figures, as both their share prices are less than 16 times earnings. If we did want to invest in the other companies, we'd have to wait either until they fell in price to a level we're happy to pay or until the next earnings update is released and we can see if the EPS has changed (updates usually come out every six months).

Dividends

Dividends are paid to shareholders out of the company's net profit. That cheque you receive from the company every six months simply for owning their shares is one of the best things about share ownership. The better a company is doing, usually the higher the dividend it'll pay its shareholders.

Not every company will pay dividends, though (it's not a requirement). Some prefer to reinvest the profits back into the company. And unless you're looking purely for income (about which more later), don't put too much emphasis on whether a company pays dividends or not — think of them as just a nice little bonus on your journey to being rich.

Investing for dividend income

Listed property trusts, in particular, can pay dividends of 8 to 10 per cent per annum, sometimes even more, and often people buy shares in them as an alternative to a high-interest bank account. Not only do you receive a decent income, the share price will increase in value as well. However, be aware that the share prices of companies that pay high dividends generally don't increase as much as those that pay lower dividends.

Share behaviour at dividend payout time

Shares can behave very strangely at times, and this is especially obvious around the date that dividends are due. When a dividend is announced, the share price will often rise significantly, and there'll be a lot of buying and selling as investors scramble to buy shares in the company before the ex-dividend date.

> **Money terms**
>
> **Ex dividend**—'without dividend'. The ex-dividend date is the date set by the company after which any shares sold aren't eligible for the dividend payment. In other words, even if you sell your shares after this date, you'll receive the full dividend; if you buy shares after this date, you won't get the dividend.

Once the ex-dividend date passes, the share price often falls rapidly as investors sell up and move on, satisfied that they're eligible for the dividend payment. Long-term investors shouldn't be too concerned with this fall, as the share price usually increases again in the weeks and months following. Still, it's an interesting phenomenon to observe.

So, how confident are you feeling now about choosing some shares to invest in? Our friend Penny Saver is ready to get going and is planning on investing $10 000. Here's her plan of attack.

Case study—Penny Saver

Amount available to invest—$10 000
Date of investment—3 November 2007

The first thing Penny does is choose some stocks to invest in using our six rules. To save research time she buys Martin Roth's *Top Stocks 2008* from the bookstore, which lists all the figures she wants to know.

1 *Choose market leaders*. Penny has decided to concentrate on the stocks listed in the All Ords Index (the top 500 stocks by market capitalisation in Australia).

2 *Choose companies with a debt-to-equity ratio of less than 75 per cent*. Since all of the companies listed in Martin's book have a debt-to-equity ratio of less than 70 per cent, Penny considers this rule met.

3 *Choose companies with a return on equity of at least 15 per cent*. One of the criteria Martin uses to select companies for his book is an ROE of at least 10 per cent, but Penny is going to stick with my rule of at

least 15 per cent. That narrows the selection down to 81 companies.

4 & 5 *Choose companies listed for five years or more, with an average return of at least 15 per cent.* Of the 81 stocks Penny has already selected, 70 of them fit this rule.

6 *Choose companies with an earnings stability of at least 80 per cent.* This is one rule that isn't listed in Martin's book, so Penny has to find it out herself, but it doesn't take long. Penny heads to her online broker's website and finds that out of the 70 companies, only the following eight have earnings stability of at least 80 per cent:

COU — Count Financial

COH — Cochlear

TNE — Technology One

WOW — Woolworths

ASX — ASX

CBA — Commonwealth Bank

WBB — Wide Bay Australia

HIL — Hills Industrials.

Price to pay: 16 times earnings

Penny now looks at these eight companies' current trading prices and their earnings per share (EPS), and puts together the figures over the page.

Company	ASX code	Current price	EPS	16 × EPS	Is price < 16 × EPS?
Count Financial	COU	$2.80	8.8¢	$1.41	No
Cochlear	COH	$69.88	180.1¢	$28.82	No
Technology One	TNE	$1.06	4.9¢	$0.78	No
Woolworths	WOW	$35.52	107.8¢	$17.25	No
ASX	ASX	$58.11	190.6¢	$30.50	No
Comm. Bank	CBA	$61.20	339.7¢	$54.35	No
Wide Bay Australia	WBB	$12.60	64.8¢	$10.37	No
Hills Industrials	HIL	$5.54	27.5¢	$4.40	No

Penny has a problem: none of these companies are trading at less than 16 times EPS! Sometimes, especially if the market is at an all-time high (which was the case in November 2007), it can be difficult to find companies trading at great prices. It's much easier to find bargains when the market has fallen a bit, or, as I like to say, when the companies go on sale.

Penny needs to decide whether she's happy to wait until the EPS figures are recalculated (in 6 to 12 months) or the share prices fall to an acceptable level — or whether she's prepared to either pay a little bit more than 16 times earnings or relax some of her other rules.

She decides that she's prepared to pay a little bit extra in order to buy now, and looks at the eight companies again to find the ones trading closest to 16 times EPS:

Company	ASX code	Current price	16 × EPS	% difference
Comm. Bank	CBA	$61.20	$54.35	11.2%
Wide Bay Australia	WBB	$12.60	$10.37	17.7%
Hills Industrials	HIL	$5.54	$4.40	20.6%
Technology One	TNE	$1.06	$0.78	26.4%
ASX	ASX	$58.11	$30.50	47.5%
Count Financial	COU	$2.80	$1.41	49.6%
Woolworths	WOW	$35.52	$17.25	51.4%
Cochlear	COH	$69.88	$28.82	58.8%

You can see from the table that the three companies trading closest to our desired 16 times EPS are Commonwealth Bank, Wide Bay Australia and Hills Industrials. Penny splits her $10 000 evenly between these three. Here are the buy orders she places through her broker:

54 × CBA shares @ $61.20 = $3304.80
263 × WBB shares @ $12.60 = $3313.80
600 × HIL shares @ $5.54 = $3324.00
3 × brokerage fees @ $19.95 each = $59.85
Total = $10002.45

How much Penny will make from her three investments is anyone's guess. (You'll have a much better idea than I do, since you're reading this book in the future and can check where the prices went.) However, she's confident that she's chosen great companies, and all she needs to do now is keep an occasional eye on things and check that the companies are still on track when their next financial statements come through.

Are you confident that you could try long-term investing too now? You've got a grasp on the basics, and it's really not as difficult as you think. The media would have people believe they need a degree in economics and an in-depth understanding of the world financial markets in order to invest, but really, as long as you stick to these simple rules, you should be fine. I don't have an economics degree, and my investment results aren't any worse for it.

11 Investing for the short term

By the end of this chapter, you'll:

- be able to do your own technical research
- know the rules for choosing short-term investment stocks.

Investing in the stock market over the short term, or 'trading' as it's often called, means making a profit from the volatile nature of the sharemarket. There's no doubt it's way more fun than long-term investing. For a start, every time you check the share prices you get a little thrill to see your shares increase in price—or you start biting your nails because the prices have fallen. (I've read plenty of books that say sensible traders shouldn't react emotionally to their shares' ups and downs—maybe that's easy if you've set a computer to make the decisions for you! I think the rest of us should feel free to do a happy dance if our shares start increasing in price, as long as we don't allow our emotions to cause us to make silly decisions.)

The length of time that a short-term investor will hold a share varies: it can be anywhere from an hour to a year. When I was short-term investing, I held shares for an average of two to three months, though once I did buy and sell some shares in just three days.

As you'd expect, the rules for choosing trading stocks are quite different to the ones for choosing investment stocks. Most traders pick stocks based on charts, economic trends, takeover and profit announcements, or a combination of all three of those things. The way I see it, short-term investing is a numbers game: some shares will increase in price and some will fall. And unfortunately, even the best research on the most likely candidates for price rises isn't guaranteed to get you a portfolio that'll land you on *BRW*'s Rich 200 list. You'll probably choose a few great companies and a few bad companies, but most will likely not do much at all. As long as you act fast to sell the stocks that fall and keep those that are rising, you should come out ahead — in other words, ride the winners, dump the losers and keep an eye on the boring ones.

All you need for short-term investing is a bit of research and a plan, and you'll be able to choose shares that have every chance of becoming profitable winners for you. So, let's have a look now at my five rules for short-term investing.

Rule #1: choose the best-performing sectors

Once you start looking at the sharemarket you'll notice that shares are often divided into sectors or categories. We looked at a couple of sectors briefly in the last chapter — the

S&P/ASX 100, for example, comprises the 100 largest stocks by market capitalisation. There are also sectors based on the type of company, including Energy, Health Care and Information Technology. These are known as GICS (Global Industry Classification Standard) sectors. The main sectors are as follows (in no particular order):

Sectors by market capitalisation

S&P/ASX 20
S&P/ASX 50
S&P/ASX 100
S&P/ASX 200
S&P/ASX 300
S&P/ASX Midcap 50
S&P/ASX Small Ordinaries
All Ordinaries

GICS sectors

S&P/ASX Consumer Discretionary
S&P/ASX Energy
S&P/ASX Financials
S&P/ASX Financial-ex-Property Trusts
S&P/ASX Health Care
S&P/ASX Industrials
S&P/ASX Information Technology
S&P/ASX Materials
S&P/ASX Property Trusts
S&P/ASX Consumer Staples
S&P/ASX Telecommunication Services
S&P/ASX Utilities

Check with your broker or use a financial website such as <http://yahoo7.com.au/finance> to find out which sectors have done well over the last three months. (You can't usually use newspapers, as they only give current prices, not past prices.) I like to put the information in a table like the one below, so I can easily work out the percentage changes.

GICS sectors

	ASX Code	01 Sep 07	% change Sept–Oct	1 Oct 07	% change Oct–Nov	01 Nov 07
Telecomm	XTJ	1554.9	–1.1%	1538.5	8.8%	1673.7
Cons Stap	XSJ	8224.8	1.0%	8304.2	6.3%	8823.3
Fin x PT	XXJ	7280.7	2.4%	7455.7	5.2%	7846.2
Materials	XMJ	13540.8	14.2%	15458.5	4.5%	16148.3
Financials	XFJ	7063.9	2.1%	7210.4	4.4%	7525.8
Industrials	XNJ	6940.8	3.4%	7178.4	4.2%	7482.8
Energy	XEJ	14271.0	10.4%	15753.3	1.9%	16058.1
Cons Dis	XDJ	2730.7	1.5%	2770.7	1.4%	2809.5
Prop Trust	XPJ	2417.8	0.9%	2440.6	1.2%	2470.7
Health	XHJ	8910.9	6.2%	9460.5	–0.4%	9424.1
Info Tech	XIJ	600.4	–8.5%	549.2	–3.2%	531.6
Utilities	XUJ	7240.9	1.0%	7316.7	–4.0%	7021.6

S&P/ASX sectors

20	TLI	3381.0	5.7%	3573.0	5.2%	3758.7
50	FLI	6078.4	5.1%	6390.0	3.9%	6636.5
100	TOI	5049.1	5.2%	5312.2	3.8%	5513.3
200	XJO	6247.2	5.1%	6563.7	4.0%	6828.7

If you look at the S&P/ASX market capitalisation sectors, you can see that the S&P/ASX 20 has outperformed the other indices in both of the two months. The GICS sectors are a little bit more volatile, but from looking at both months, my pick for top-performing sector would be Materials, which increased 14.2 per cent from 1 September 2007 to 1 October 2007 and 4.5 per cent from 1 October 2007 to 1 November 2007.

Next, I'd probably choose Industrials and 'Fin x PT' (which stands for 'Financials Excluding Property Trusts'), as they've shown the most consistency. Even though some of the other sectors have done better in a one-month period, I'd still go with those three sectors because of their consistency from month to month.

Rule #2: choose the top companies within the best sectors

Now that I've picked the top-performing sectors, I can choose the top-performing companies from those sectors. You can get a list of the companies that make up the sectors fairly easily from your broker, any financial website or even from the newspaper.

Have a look to see which of the companies have performed best over the last three months. The easiest way to do this is to create a simple table listing all the price figures, which you can get from your charting software, if you have some, or from Yahoo! Finance (see the box over the page for more).

Shhh! Fast-track your research

Yahoo! Finance has a nifty tool for finding the past prices for any share. Just go to <http://yahoo7.com.au/finance> , enter the code for the company in the 'Enter symbol(s)' search box and click 'Go', then click the 'Historical Prices' link in the left-hand navigation bar that comes up, and enter the dates you're interested in. Voila! Quick past prices. You can choose any start and end date you like and get daily, weekly or monthly prices. This is what the screen looks like:

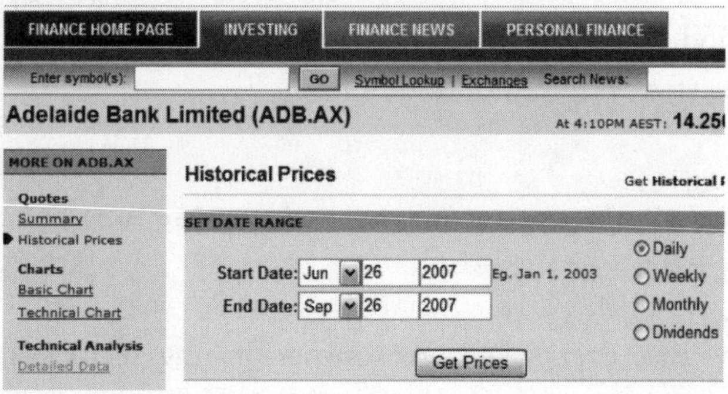

Reproduced with the permission of Yahoo!7

After some searching, you should have a list of about 10 of the best performers in the best sectors that looks something like the table opposite.

I've only looked at the stocks within the Materials sector for this example, since it was shown to be the best performer, but you can use any or all of your top three sectors.

Best performers within the Materials sector over two months

Code	Price at 3 Nov 07	Increase from previous month	Price at 3 Oct 07	Increase from previous month	Price at 3 Sep 07
JBM	$23.55	47.2%	$16.00	6.2%	$15.07
PNA	$1.115	34.3%	$0.83	22.1%	$0.68
MCC	$8.09	28.4%	$6.30	–9.0%	$6.92
GNS	$3.83	26.8%	$3.02	–8.2%	$3.29
SMY	$5.89	22.2%	$4.82	17.0%	$4.12
NCM	$32.70	18.0%	$27.71	13.6%	$24.40
MGX	$2.79	17.2%	$2.38	50.6%	$1.58
NUF	$15.60	13.9%	$13.70	–3.5%	$14.20
MCR	$4.85	13.1%	$4.29	15.6%	$3.71
WSA	$5.93	13.0%	$5.25	16.7%	$4.50

Before I do anything else, I'm going to remove the stocks that fell during either of the two months. Next, I'll look at the performance of the remaining stocks. As you can see, many did well in October but performed poorly in September. Jubilee Mines (JBM), for instance, increased by a whopping 47.2 per cent in the month to 3 November, but only 6.2 per cent the previous month. Now, while this looks great (and would have been great if you'd held the share during that time), I'm not convinced it will keep up, so I might just tuck Jubilee away and look at it again in a few months. I'm interested in consistency — stocks that perform around the same month to month.

Here are the stocks left over after my cull (I like to call it panning for gold, as the dirt falls away and you're left with the nuggets):

Code	Price at 3 Nov 07	Increase from previous month	Price at 3 Oct 07	Increase from previous month	Price at 3 Sep 07
PNA	$1.115	34.3%	$0.83	22.1%	$0.68
SMY	$5.89	22.2%	$4.82	17.0%	$4.12
NCM	$32.70	18.0%	$27.71	13.6%	$24.40
MCR	$4.85	13.1%	$4.29	15.6%	$3.71
WSA	$5.93	13.0%	$5.25	16.7%	$4.50

They all increased by roughly the same amount in each of the two months. Of course, that's no guarantee that they'll do well in the future, but I feel more confident knowing I've done my best to choose the most promising companies.

Rule #3: choose shares in an uptrend

So far things have been pretty straightforward, but now that we've narrowed down our selections to a handful of companies, we need to take an even closer look at what the shares are doing. To do this, we're going to use the most common method of determining a share's pattern — so let's talk charts.

Charting, or technical analysis, is plotting the price history of a share over a period of time. The idea behind it is that, by looking at a graphical representation of the numbers over time, you'll be able to spot what the share is doing and, hopefully, predict what it will do in the future. At its most basic, if the share is in an uptrend (going up in price), you buy; if it starts a downtrend (decreases in price), you sell.

The most useful charts, I think, are the 'candlestick' charts, so named because the bars look like candles with wicks at both ends, as you can see in the diagram. They not only give you information about the price of a share at the close of the market, but also the price it opened at and its highest and lowest price during the period. A white candlestick means the price ended higher than it started; a black or coloured candlestick means it ended the period lower—as you can see in the Westpac chart below, which shows Westpac's daily price movements over three months.

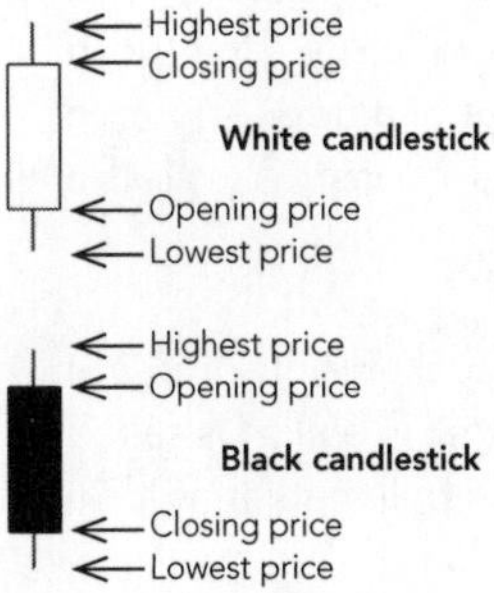

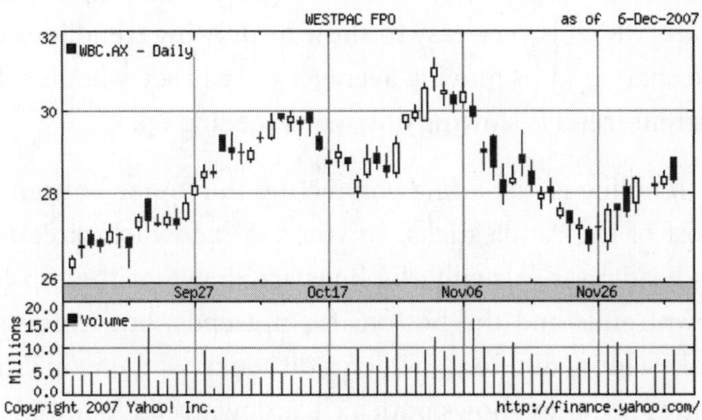

Reproduced with permission of Yahoo! Inc. © 2007 by Yahoo! Inc. YAHOO! and the YAHOO! logo are trademarks of Yahoo! Inc.

Generally, the more white candlesticks there are, the more likely the share is bullish, and you should buy it (or hold if you already have it). If there are a lot of black candlesticks, then the share is bearish.

Money terms

Bearish—(A sharemarket or an individual stock) Falling or being considered likely to fall in price. The term is thought to have originated from traders who sold their bear skins with the expectations that prices would fall in the future. I prefer to think of a big grumpy grizzly bear falling out of a tree—nothing good can come of that! A market that is *bearish* is called a *bear market.*

Bullish—(A sharemarket or an individual stock) Rising or being considered likely to rise in price. A market that is *bullish* is called a *bull market.* Obviously you want to be in a bull market as long as possible.

When it comes to charting, I prefer to keep things simple. The main things I look for are the general direction of the share, which is very easy to show by drawing trendlines on the chart, and its moving average, so I can see whether the current trend is slowing down or speeding up.

A trendline is just a line connecting the top or bottom of most of the candlesticks, so you can see which direction it's heading in. Usually the lines are drawn at the top for downtrends and the bottom for uptrends, but it doesn't make a lot of difference which side you draw them on. This chart for Caltex shows both a clear downtrend followed by an uptrend, both marked with trendlines.

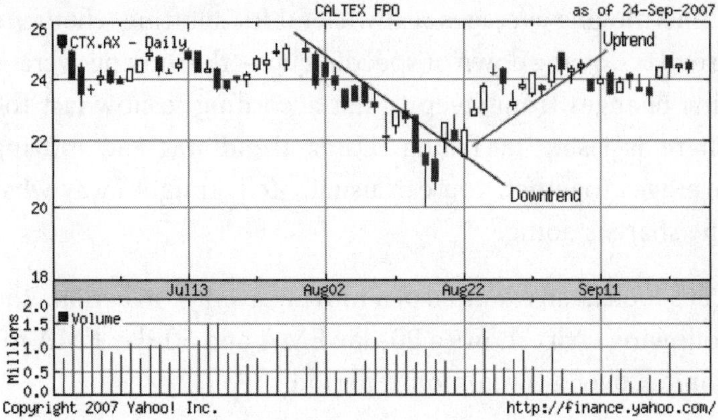

Reproduced with permission of Yahoo! Inc. © 2007 by Yahoo! Inc. YAHOO! and the YAHOO! logo are trademarks of Yahoo! Inc.

Using a trendline you can tell pretty quickly what direction the share's heading in — and even more importantly, when that trend is about to change. In this example, it would have been good to buy when the share price rose clearly above the downtrend line, and sell when it dropped through the uptrend line. If you'd invested $5000 in this way, you could have bought 225 shares at around $22.20 and sold them at around $23.80, making a profit of $360 in three weeks.

You can plot a moving average onto a chart using a charting program, the ASX website or any of your other favourite financial websites. A moving average is the sum of the closing prices of the company over a set period, averaged into a line on the chart. The two most common types of moving average are the simple moving average (SMA) and the exponential moving average (EMA). The SMA gives equal weight to each price over the period, whereas the EMA gives more weight to the most recent prices. I like to stick with 15-day or 30-day moving averages, but feel free to choose whichever time frame suits you.

I find moving averages really useful for spotting whether a trend is slowing down or speeding up — the moving average line changes from steep to flat according to how fast the share is rising or falling. Using trendlines and moving averages together, you can usually tell straight away what the share is doing.

Let's look at an example of a moving average in action. The following chart shows a 20-day EMA and 50-day EMA for Zinifex over a three-month period.

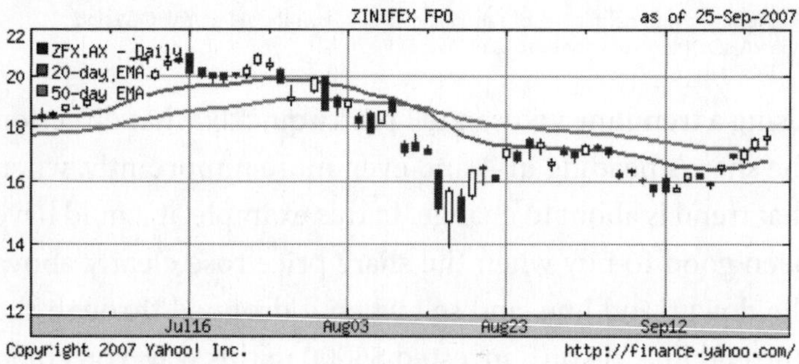

Reproduced with permission of Yahoo! Inc. © 2007 by Yahoo! Inc. YAHOO! and the YAHOO! logo are trademarks of Yahoo! Inc.

You can see an interesting movement on this chart at around 10 August: the 20-day EMA crosses and falls below the 50-day EMA. This is an extremely bearish sign called a 'dead cross', and you can see that the price fell quite soon after it. If the 20-day EMA were to cross back up through the 50-day EMA at some point (a 'golden cross'), it would be a good sign that the share is due for a turnaround, and might signal the start of an uptrend. If all the other signs were favourable, it might then be worth buying some shares.

Let's go back to the five companies I picked out using rule #2, and have a quick look at their charts to see which ones we could consider purchasing. We'll use a three-month candlestick chart with a 20-day EMA for all of them, so that we can compare them equally.

Here's the chart for Pan Australian Resources (PNA). As you can see, it's been trading upwards and has been above the moving average since around 22 August. It certainly looks like a good contender!

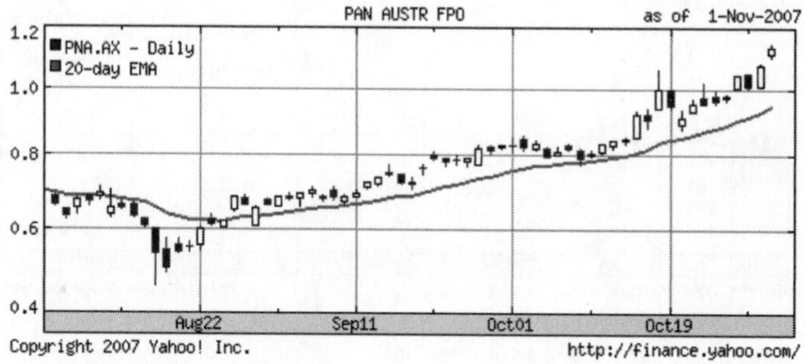

Reproduced with permission of Yahoo! Inc. © 2007 by Yahoo! Inc. YAHOO! and the YAHOO! logo are trademarks of Yahoo! Inc.

Sally Malay Mining (SMY) looks pretty good, too. It's also trending upwards, and although it's had a few dips below its 20-day EMA, it seems to recover nicely each time.

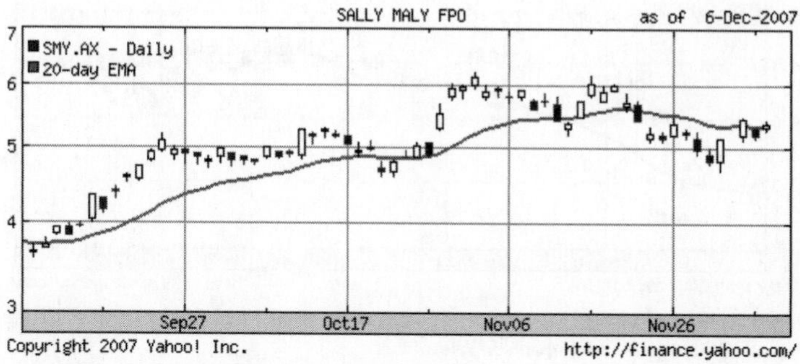

Reproduced with permission of Yahoo! Inc. © 2007 by Yahoo! Inc. YAHOO! and the YAHOO! logo are trademarks of Yahoo! Inc.

The next chart is of Newcrest Mining Limited (NCM). It's also moving fairly close to its 20-day EMA, and has been in an uptrend since around 15 September. It looks like it had been in a sideways pattern before it broke out around 12 September — notice the strange candlestick pattern around that time.

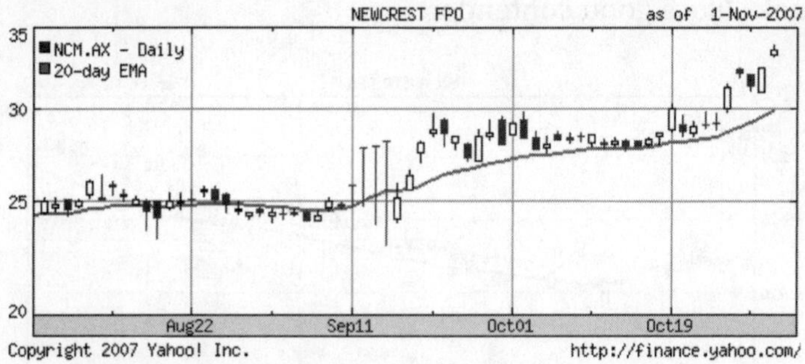

Reproduced with permission of Yahoo! Inc. © 2007 by Yahoo! Inc. YAHOO! and the YAHOO! logo are trademarks of Yahoo! Inc.

Mincor Resources (MCR) has also only recently broken through its 20-day EMA and looks to be on the rise. Before that it was in a downtrend.

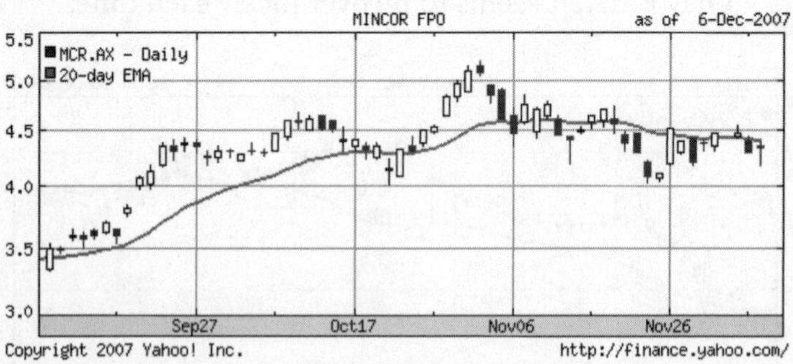

Reproduced with permission of Yahoo! Inc. © 2007 by Yahoo! Inc. YAHOO! and the YAHOO! logo are trademarks of Yahoo! Inc.

My last pick, Western Areas (WSA), shows the most volatility of all the five stocks. Looking at a longer time frame might give a clearer idea of where it is going, but for now, I'd probably put this one on the bottom of the list.

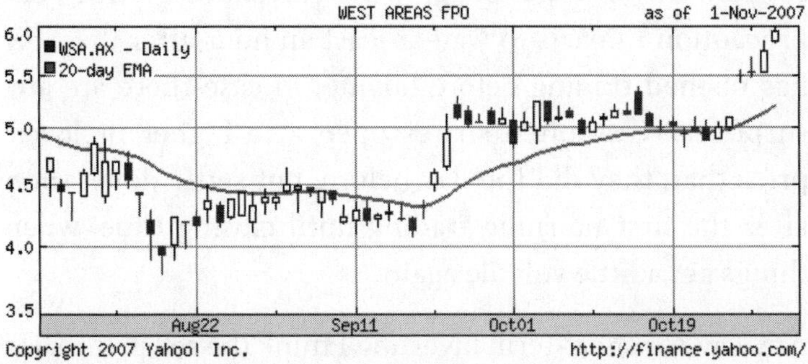

Reproduced with permission of Yahoo! Inc. © 2007 by Yahoo! Inc. YAHOO! and the YAHOO! logo are trademarks of Yahoo! Inc.

Rule #4: choose the most consistent companies

Even when it comes to short-term investing, I like to keep surprises to a minimum. So once I've chosen a handful of companies and checked out their charts to see which are in strong uptrends, I also find out which are the most consistent month by month.

We've already checked the five companies' figures for the previous two months and looked at their charts to see which seems most consistent. Taking both charts and figures into account, I'd pick these three companies as the most consistent:

PNA—Pan Australian Resources
NCM—Newcrest Mining
SMY—Sally Malay Mining

The only thing left to do now is place a buy order for one of them! I wouldn't get too hung up on the price you buy at; if the share is in an uptrend, it's likely that you'll miss out altogether if you try to buy at a particular price. Just set your buy order to roughly the current price. The only precaution I take is to wait at least an hour after the ASX has opened trading before buying, in case there are any surprises. Very often shares open at a higher or lower price than they did the day before, but settle down soon after the first morning trading until closing time, when things get a little volatile again.

Anyway, for short-term investing I think the sell price is far more important than the buy price. The sell price determines how much profit you'll make (or how much loss you'll cop): read rule #5 to find out how to maximise your profit.

Rule #5: set the price you'll sell at, now

When you make a short-term investment, you need to set your escape route at the start — that is, decide at what point you'll exit the share for good or ill. I like to set my sell price as soon as I've bought the shares; in fact, I usually set two sell prices and a time limit straight away. The first is my stop-loss sell price.

Money terms

Stop loss — A price set ahead of time at which you intend to sell your shares to minimise losses.

Stop losses

There have been times when I've been so sure about a share, but as soon as I buy it, it falls in price! It's almost as if it knew I'd just bought it and fell to spite me. It's important to give yourself some 'insurance' to minimise losing all your money on a share like that. I usually set a stop loss around 10 per cent below the price that I paid for the share, so that the most I can ever lose on that company is just 10 per cent. The reason I choose 10 per cent is because it's about equivalent to my level of anxiety if the share does fall!

The fear most people have about the stock market is that they'll lose all of their money. Setting a stop loss means you don't have to worry about that anymore — if the price does fall, you'll have an out. If you set your stop losses at 10 per cent below the price you paid, like I do, then most of your capital will remain intact, and you can choose a better company to invest in to try and get back the little you lost.

I don't go under 10 per cent, simply to give the share some breathing room. As you've seen by looking at charts, even when the share is in an uptrend, it never moves in a straight line. It might be high one day, low the next; it's the overall pattern we're concerned with. Setting your stop loss at too low a percentage might mean you sell out of the share when it's just doing its usual movements, and if you do that, you'll miss the profit when it does increase again.

It's important to be strong and stick to your stop loss. Too often people hold on just that bit longer to see if the share will go back up, and in my opinion, that's a mistake. If it doesn't go back up, then you'll lose even more money.

If you're really convinced the share will pick up again, sell at your stop-loss price anyway. Just keep a close eye on the share and buy it back later if the signs point to a turnaround.

Profit sell prices

The second sell price I set is my profit sell. This is the price that I expect the share to rise to over the time I'm prepared to hold it. So, for example, if the share has averaged a 4 per cent rise every month for the last three months, I might expect it to do the same over the next three months. I would therefore set my profit sell to around 12 per cent (4 per cent × 3 months) higher than the price I paid.

Example — Pan Australian Resources

We can look at stop losses and profit sell prices in more detail with the shares that I've already chosen. Pan Australian Resources (PNA) is currently trading at 1.115 (yes, lower priced shares can trade at half-cents: the extra 0.005 is not a typing error). I've set my stop loss at around 10 per cent lower, making it $1.00. The average increase for PNA over the previous two months was 56.4 per cent (34.3 per cent + 22.1 per cent). So I've set my profit sell at $1.74 (1.115 × 56.4 per cent). I did the same for the next two companies.

Now, the average increases for these shares do seem very high, so it might be unrealistic to expect them to continue like this (but never say never). To make sure that you still make a profit but keep things realistic, you could try using a trailing stop loss instead of a profit sell.

Code	Price at 3 Nov 07	Stop loss (10% less than current price)	Average % increase over last 2 months	Profit sell
PNA	$1.115	$1.00	56.4%	$1.74
SMY	$5.89	$5.30	39.2%	$8.20
NCM	$32.70	$29.43	31.6%	$43.03

Trailing stop losses

A trailing stop loss is where your stop loss moves up as the share price moves up, the theory being that this protects your profits. I've started to like trailing stops better than simply setting a fixed profit sell price, as they mean I don't jump out too early if the share is in for a huge ride upwards—I'm quite happy to go along and enjoy its journey.

Let's say that you were interested in CSL and purchased 60 shares on 29 June 2007 for $88 each (total invested = 60 × $88 = $5280). You immediately set your initial stop-loss price to 10 per cent below your buy price, at $79.20: if the share falls below this point you will sell.

Date	CSL price	Stop loss
29 June 07	$88.00	$79.20

Recalculate your stop loss every month to make sure everything's still on track. On 27 July, the closing price is $87.65. A smidgeon below what you paid for it, but certainly nothing to worry about. Don't change your stop loss at this point, as a stop loss can only trail upwards if the price goes higher; if the price is lower, it remains fixed.

Date	CSL price	Stop loss	
29 June 07	$88.00	$79.20	
27 July 07	$87.65	$79.20	(remains fixed at last price)

By 29 August, the share has increased in value to $96.33. A great little increase over the month, and you move your stop loss to 10 per cent below that price so it's now set at $86.70. If the share falls below $86.70 from now on, you'll immediately sell; otherwise you'll keep holding the share.

Date	CSL price	Stop loss	
29 June 07	$88.00	$79.20	
27 July 07	$87.65	$79.20	(remains fixed at last price)
29 Aug 07	$96.33	$86.70	(10% below current price)

By 28 September, the share has had another great increase and the price is $107.30. So, again, you move the stop loss to 10 per cent below the current price, bringing it to $96.57. As you can see, the stop loss is now above the price you originally paid for it, meaning that even if the share took a turn for the worse tomorrow, you'd sell at $96.57 and still make a decent profit! Using a trailing stop loss, as long as the share is increasing in price, you are guaranteed of making a profit.

Date	CSL price	Stop loss	
29 June 07	$88.00	$79.20	
27 July 07	$87.65	$79.20	(remains fixed at last price)
29 Aug 07	$96.33	$86.70	(10% below current price)
28 Sep 07	$107.30	$96.57	

If you were using a fixed profit sell price, you might have sold the share by now and cashed in your profit. And you might have sold too early and missed jumps in the price. So, each time the share rises, just adjust your stop-loss point upwards. If the share falls in price, keep your stop loss at its current price. If it falls to your current stop loss, sell at that price or as close to it as the market will pay.

On 16 October, the stock falls and hits the stop-loss price, causing an automatic sell. By selling out at that price of $96.57, you would have made the following profit:

Original investment—$5280 (60 × $88.00)
Sold for $5794.20—(60 × $96.57)
Profit—$514.20, or just under 10 per cent in 4 months

Time frame limit

The last limit I usually set is a time frame. Setting a time frame for holding the share is good—it means you aren't stuck with a share that's just going sideways, and you can put your money into better investments.

Usually, I put a time limit of around three months on my short-term investments. If the share doesn't move much within three months, I'll sell it and put my money into something more profitable. There's no use holding onto a stock that's going nowhere! Of course, if it's increasing in price and moving my trailing stop loss up, I'll keep holding onto it.

Now, let's check in with Penny and see how she's going with her short-term investing.

Case study—Penny Saver

Penny has $10 000 in the bank, and has decided to try short-term investing over the next five months. She decides to invest $2000 this month, $2000 the next month and so forth. The reason she's decided to do this is so she can diversify her portfolio and hopefully hold a number of different stocks over different sectors. Each month she'll do her research using our five rules to determine which sector and company is the best to invest in.

This month, she's going to choose one of the stocks from the ASX Materials sector, since we already did the research for her. From the three we've chosen, she settles on Newcrest Mining (NCM), and buys 61 shares at $32.70 each. She has decided to use a trailing stop loss rather than try to choose a fixed profit sell price.

Buy: 61 NCM × $32.70 = $1994.70

Date	NCM price	Stop loss
3 Nov 07	$32.70	$29.43

At the start of December, she'll choose a new sector and company to invest in, and so on; after five months, she should have a diversified portfolio of short-term stocks.

12 Investing in property

By the end of this chapter, you'll know:

- why you should consider investing in property
- how to apply for a loan
- what checks you need to do before you sign the contract.

There's nothing I like more than sitting down and watching a property renovation show on television. I love how they can turn a tired old room that looks like it hasn't been touched since the 1970s into something modern and elegant. They always make such a difference and increase the value of the property by an outstanding amount.

Of course, when I splash a bright colour on my walls it always seems to look more *Play School* than *Home Beautiful*. But there's no question that if you've got the time, patience and creativity, there's money to be made in renovation.

There are three main ways that people make money from property:

- sell the property for more than you paid (either because it's increased in value over time or because another buyer is willing to pay more for it now)
- renovate it so that the price increases in value
- rent it out and collect the rental income.

The beauty of investing in real estate is that if you buy smart in the beginning, you're very likely to make a decent profit, because real estate is generally a pretty stable investment choice. After all, a house isn't like a company that could go belly up — bricks and mortar generally doesn't disappear unless there's a major catastrophe such as fire, flood or Cyclone Sally, and even then you'll no doubt have insurance to cover your losses.

Yes, I know, I've heard all the stories about little old ladies who were suckered into buying an investment unit on the Gold Coast for triple its value. If you're smart about choosing the right place and check out values and comparable property in the area, you can be fairly confident that your investment will reap you great rewards.

Historically, property investors have done remarkably well in the capital cities of Australia, with the average home doubling in value every seven to nine years:

- Sydney has had annual growth of 9.45 per cent over the last 45 years. That means the average house doubled in value every seven to eight years.

- Melbourne's growth rate since 1960 has been 8.75 per cent, meaning house prices doubled on average every eight years.
- Brisbane has a recorded growth of 9.14 per cent over the past 21 years, which means houses doubled in price around every eight years.
- Adelaide and Perth's growth rates would see your house value double every nine years.
- In Canberra, your house would double in value every eight years.
- Hobart has had an annual growth rate of around 8.2 per cent since 1984, meaning prices doubled every eight to nine years.
- Darwin had the lowest growth of all the capital cities, but actually had the highest yield (rental return). So even though property took longer to double in value, the good yields made up for it.

Source: 'How Long Does It Take to Double Your Money?', Natalie Powell, 20/04/2007, <Propertyupdate.com.au>

As you can see, the return on property is historically lower than the return on shares — but then the risk is a lot lower as well. The reason people get so excited about investing in property is that you can leverage your investment and potentially make much more money that you put in. True, you can leverage shares as well by buying them on margin, but it's much more common to leverage property — in fact almost everyone does, because it's rare to be able to afford a house or shop or factory with cash!

> **Money terms**
>
> **Leverage**—To borrow money to purchase an investment, and therefore to increase your rate of return.

Let's go through the benefits you'd get from leverage if you, say, bought an investment property in Sydney for $500 000, paid a 20 per cent deposit ($100 000) and borrowed the rest from the bank. To keep the example simple, we'll imagine that you took out an interest-only loan (more on these later) of 7.25 per cent on the $400 000 balance.

After seven years, the value of the property has doubled to $1 000 000. The amount of money that you put into the investment to begin with was $100 000, and you paid approximately $202 944 in interest over the seven years (based on monthly repayments of $2416 × 12 months × 7 years). If you could sell your property now for $1 000 000 and pay off the $400 000 loan (you didn't pay back any principal to the bank, only the interest, so you still owe the bank the full amount), you'd be left with $600 000 in your pocket. Deduct the interest that you paid the bank (just over $200 000) and you find that the actual profit you made on the property was around $400 000! Not bad for an initial $100 000 investment.

I'll discuss all the three ways of making money from real estate in more detail, but first, let's look at the things that are common to all investment strategies. Whether you're planning to renovate, hold the place long term or rent it out, you've still got to work out how much you can afford to borrow, find the perfect property, get all the checks done, get a loan and get insurance.

How much can you borrow?

Visit the website of any financial institution that deals in home loans and you can play with little calculators that tell you how much you might be able to borrow and what the repayments might be. Some even do nifty things like show you how much money you could save by paying fortnightly instead of monthly or by paying extra lump sums into the loan. However, these are just guides. When you actually go into a bank to apply for a loan, the amount they offer may be very different.

The amount the bank or financial institution will lend you depends on a number of things. First and foremost is how much you earn — the bank needs to know that you'll have a regular income and can afford the loan repayments. Second, they'll want to know how stable your income is — being in your job for more than a year is usually good enough, but longer is generally better.

Third, they'll look to see if you have other debts such as credit cards or car and personal loans. While it's still possible to get a property loan if you have personal debt, usually the amount they'll lend you will be reduced, so it's a good idea to pay your debt off before you apply for a property loan. As a bonus, paying off a debt fast will usually give your credit rating a boost, so the bank managers will be knocking down your door to offer you a loan.

Last, they'll check if you've got any savings, investments or other assets that will also show that you're a good loan candidate. Sometimes it's not necessary to have a deposit saved to be eligible for a loan, as there are plenty of 100 per cent financing deals around. However, if you want to avoid the often-expensive mortgage insurance, it's a good idea to have 20 per cent or more of the property's value saved to use as a deposit.

Money terms

Lender's mortgage insurance (LMI)—This is not to be confused with home and contents insurance (which you need) or mortgage protection insurance (which covers your payments if you are injured or lose your job). Mortgage insurance is what the bank makes you take out to cover them in case you can't pay back the loan. Usually only people with no deposit or a low deposit have to take it out. It's best avoided if possible, because it can be very expensive (often thousands of dollars) and it's there for the bank's benefit, not yours.

Once the bank tells you how much they're willing to lend you, I want you to go away and ask yourself if you can really afford that much. Usually, when people get into trouble paying their loans, it's because they've overextended themselves with a big mortgage. Just because the bank says you can borrow $700 000 doesn't necessarily mean that you should!

You worked out a budget in the earlier chapters in this book (you *did* do your budget, right?), so you know how much you can afford to pay on a home loan each month. Base how much you decide to borrow on this figure. It's also a good idea to calculate whether you could still comfortably afford the repayments if the loan's interest rate rose 2 to 3 per cent higher. You want to leave some breathing room.

First homebuyers

If you've never owned property in your name before and plan on living in the property that you buy, then you'll probably be eligible for the First Home Owner Grant of $7000. This government grant was set up to help buyers with their first home, regardless of the income they earn or assets they own. The government also offers the First Home Plus initiative, which provides exemptions or concessions on transfer duty and mortgage duty.

The states are responsible for administering these schemes, but your bank or financial institution should have all the forms you need to apply, and will usually give you them in a bundle with all their forms (yes, there's a lot of paperwork involved in buying a house). If not, you can get the forms from your state's revenue office or download them from the office's website. Then, all you need to do is submit your forms and your mortgage document when you lodge your Agreement for Sale/Transfer with the revenue office.

What loan and loan term should I get?

Basic variable, standard variable, low rate, fixed rate, no doc, split—phew! No wonder people are confused over which home loan they should get.

To be honest, most of them are pretty similar. The main difference is whether the interest rate remains the same (fixed) or changes over time according to the interest rates set by the Reserve Bank (variable). The other differences usually relate to the amount of flexibility in the loan, particularly whether you can withdraw money out of the loan or put more in on top of your repayments. Here are some quick definitions of the main types of loans, so that you're better armed for the talk with your bank manager:

- *Standard variable.* This is the most popular type of home loan in Australia, and as the name suggests, the interest rate is variable. If interest rates go up, so will your repayments; if interest rates go down, your repayments will also follow. These loans are usually quite flexible, in that you can put in more money to pay off your loan quicker and can redraw funds if you need to.

- *Basic variable.* This classic no-frills loan is similar to a standard variable loan, but usually has more restrictions. Sometimes the interest rate is lower on a basic variable loan to make up for this.

- *Fixed rate.* In this type of loan, you can lock in an interest rate for anything from 6 months to 10 years. Usually these loans have higher interest rates than variable loans, and if interest rates decrease, you might be locked in at a higher rate than everyone else. Still, if you don't like surprises, this kind of loan might be for you, as you won't need to worry if market rates increase.

- *Split loan.* If you want the best of both worlds, you can split your loan so that half is fixed and half is variable. You can also get extra features like redraw and the ability to make extra payments.
- *Honeymoon rate loan.* No, this isn't a loan for newly married couples. 'Honeymoon' just means that the interest rate is lower for the first year of the loan. Once the year is up, the loan usually reverts to a standard variable type.
- *Line of credit/equity loan.* A line of credit loan allows you full access to your money so that you can withdraw or deposit as you please. The benefit is that you aren't locked into a regular repayment, but this can be a disadvantage if you are the type to 'forget' to pay off the home loan.
- *Interest-only loan.* Popular with investors, interest-only loans can be fixed or variable. The difference is you're only paying off the interest, instead of both the principal and the interest. People usually take out these loans when they're relying on time and capital gains to increase the value of the property, which they then sell.
- *Other loans.* There are many other types of loans, but they're just variations on the seven I've covered above. No doc or low doc loans are just loans available to people who might not qualify for a regular loan. No deposit loans are for people with no savings or deposit. As you might guess, the interest rate on these kinds of loans is higher.

So which loan do you need? It really depends on your financial situation, so I recommend you get advice based on your circumstances from your bank manager or financial adviser. Among other things, which loan is best for you depends on whether you're planning to live in the property or rent it out. Obviously, an investor who plans on reselling a property in six months will prefer an interest-only loan to a honeymoon loan (which usually has penalties for closing out the loan in under three to four years). But a honeymoon loan might be just right for someone who plans on living in the property for many years.

The term you take the loan out for can also make a big difference in your repayments and how much interest you pay. The standard term for a property loan is between 20 and 30 years, although you can take a shorter term if you wish. Let's check out the same loan over different time periods to see the difference this would make. We'll assume all the loans are principal and interest loans for $500 000 and have a current interest rate of 7.25 per cent.

Term	Monthly repayments	Total interest over term
30 years	$3410.88	$727 917.30
25 years	$3641.03	$584 210.30
20 years	$3951.88	$448 451.18
15 years	$4564.31	$321 576.59
10 years	$5870.05	$204 406.25

As you'd imagine, the repayments on a shorter-term loan are much higher than those on the maximum 30-year loan, but you don't pay nearly as much to the bank in interest. If you take out a loan for the maximum term of 30 years, you'll often pay more in interest than you paid for the house in the first place! Looking at the table above, for example, you can see that if you took a 25-year loan instead of a 30-year loan, your repayments would be $230 more per month, but you'd save yourself over $143 000 in interest!

Visiting the bank manager

Okay, you've got all the loan info you need. It's time to actually step into the bank or financial institution and talk to someone. Don't worry, it's not as scary as you might think: believe it or not they actually *want* to lend you money, so you'll pay them all that interest. Applying for a loan is just a matter of filling out a lot of paperwork.

I recommend looking around at a few banks and lenders to check their rates before you decide on one. You can easily do this online by visiting their websites, or you could go to a mortgage broker, who will compare home loans from many different banks and lenders for you.

Next, set up an appointment with your preferred lender to talk about their home loans. Sometimes you don't even need an appointment, you can just walk in off the street, but I recommend that you make one anyway. At this meeting, the bank rep will basically go over your loan options, then let you know how much you can borrow and how much the repayments will be.

If you're buying at auction, you'll need to have your loan sorted out before you bid. What you do is apply for and secure the loan, so that when you find the property you want, all that needs to be done is to draw down the funds.

> **Bank speak**
>
> **Securing a loan**—Being approved for a loan, sometimes before you've found a property to buy.
>
> **Drawing down**—Having the loan amount deposited in your loan account, so you can use it to pay for a property.

Finding your property

Once you've chosen a loan that suits your needs, decided how much you can afford and talked to the bank about it, the next thing to do is start looking at properties. The best place to begin is online at property websites such as <www.domain.com.au> or <www.realestate.com.au>, or you can read the ads in the real estate section of your newspaper. This will give you a good idea of the types of properties that fit your budget. You'll probably notice that most properties have set open house times when you can visit and have a stickybeak (actually, this is fun to do even if you're not looking to buy), so circle a few and go check them out.

Another good way to find properties for sale is through the actual real estate agents in your area; you can either browse the photos in their windows or go in and ask to see properties that fit your budget and requirements.

Once you've got a list of around five to 10 potentials, go out there and view them. You can get an idea of a property from photographs and a description, but nothing beats visiting the property itself. It's best to clear a few Saturdays in your calendar, as it's unlikely that you'll find the perfect place on the first weekend.

After you've seen about a dozen properties, they all start blurring into one another. It's a good idea to take a notepad and jot down things about each place that you liked and didn't like after you visit it. Some people even take photos to jog their memory, but I don't think you need to go that far. There are usually photos in the paper or online if you really need a visual reminder.

Pretty soon you'll start to home in on what you really want, and after a few weeks of looking, maybe two or three places will really stand out to you. The next step is to check them out further to make sure that they're structurally sound and everything is aboveboard legally.

Checks

Before you sign any contracts, it's wise to do your due diligence.

Is it financially viable?

You need to see lots of properties before you decide on one, so you can gauge whether the asking price is reasonable compared to similar properties on the market. It'll also help you spot an exceptional deal when one comes along, as you'll start to get an eye for what makes a good buy.

Just a word of warning. Lots of people buy properties from the heart and not the head. If you're buying a place for yourself to live in, by all means look for somewhere you love, but this chapter is primarily about investing. You need to realise that a property that makes a good home for you is not necessarily going to be the right property for making money.

If you're buying to invest, you'll need to make sure that the property is going to be profitable, so you're going to have to be a little strict on yourself. A heated lap pool doesn't make a place a good investment — lap pools can be expensive to fix if tenants start throwing furniture and beer cans in them. If a place with a lap pool does make financial sense, then by all means add it to your list — but no matter how gorgeous it is, if the figures don't add up, it's time to move on.

So how do you choose which properties are going to make you more money than others? Different things matter in different areas — fireplaces generally don't do well in places like Far North Queensland, where it never gets cold, for example, but are highly desirable in cold parts of the country. However, there are a few things that most profitable properties seem to have in common:

- *Location*. You've all heard it before: where the property is located is going to add or detract value. A property by the beach, for example, is usually a lot more expensive than a property next to a busy road, even if it's exactly the same house.
- *Facilities*. Properties close to transport, shops, schools and parks do better than those further away.

- *Type of property.* Houses quite often rise more in price than units and flats.
- *Size.* Three- or four-bedroom places are more desirable and therefore increase in price quicker than one- or two-bedroom properties. And properties with a yard or garden do better than those without.

Most of this is common sense, and by looking at properties in your area of interest you'll get an idea of what types of places sell best.

Money terms

Due diligence—The process of investigating all the details of a potential investment to make sure it's worthy of investing in.

Contract of sale—The paperwork prepared by the agent or vendor's solicitor that outlines the offer, date of settlement and any conditions that must be met before a sale is finalised.

Building inspections

The next thing you want to do is make sure that the property isn't infested with termites or about to fall down or anything. It's smart to get a building inspector or engineer to do a thorough examination before you even think of making an offer. Some people prefer to wait until they've made an offer and just put it in the contract of sale that the offer is subject to an acceptable building report. That's fine, but I think you have more negotiating power if you do the checks beforehand. Also, if the reports come back and the place *is* infested with termites, you can easily turn away and find something else.

Having said that, it usually costs around $200 to $500 to get a building inspection done, so only do them on properties that you are actually interested in purchasing. Sometimes a building inspector will also advise on pest damage, but if not, you'll need to hire a licensed pest inspector as well.

The report is bound to come back with *some* structural or building problems (especially if the property is 20 or more years old), but minor problems are usually nothing to be too concerned about. If you still want to go ahead after you get your report, use these minor issues as your negotiating points to get a lower price. You'll have a much better chance of negotiating successfully if you can cite actual faults.

The exception to this is, of course, when you're buying at auction. You can't negotiate while the auctioneer is yelling 'Any more bids?' at the top of his voice—though there's nothing to stop you making an offer on the property before auction day. Many a property never makes it to auction because the owners get a tempting offer beforehand.

Conveyancing

Next, you need to get a property solicitor or conveyancer on your team, if you haven't already. Once you make an offer and it's accepted, you'll need to pass the contract over to this person so that the conveyancing work can begin. This involves doing all the document checks on the property, like checking and preparing the sales contract and mortgage documents and checking with council to make sure no highways are due to be built at your front door, that sort of thing.

It is possible to do the conveyancing work yourself, and there are a number of do-it-yourself kits on the market, but I strongly urge you to get it done by a professional. If you make a mistake, you won't be covered by professional indemnity insurance (unlike a licensed conveyancer or solicitor), and it could cost you a lot of money. It's simply not worth saving a few hundred dollars when you're risking hundreds of thousands.

Money terms

Indemnity insurance—If any financial loss arises from a mistake in the advice of a professional (the lawyer or conveyancer, in this case), this insurance covers them for any compensation to be paid to the third party. Basically it means that if they stuff up, you'll be compensated.

Insurance

Once you've bought a property, before you ring anyone, even your mum, you must arrange insurance for the place for the period until settlement. Even if you don't have the keys yet, you need to make sure you're covered for anything that happens to the property before you walk in the door. It would be awful to find out on moving day that a cyclone knocked down the back shed a week after you signed the contract.

All you need to do is ring your insurance agent and ask for a cover note on the property from the purchase until the date of settlement. Then, when you move in, you can upgrade this to full home and contents insurance.

Other fees

When you buy a property, you aren't just hit with the property and loan payments: there are also a number of other fees. The biggest of these will be the stamp duty on your property, followed by the stamp duty on your mortgage. Yep, that's right: the government wants a piece of the action when you buy a place. If you're a first homebuyer and you meet certain criteria, you might be eligible for a concession or exemption on the stamp duty; otherwise expect to write out a very large cheque to the government.

There are also fees for registering your property, registering your mortgage and doing a title search, and sometimes the bank will slug you a few hundred dollars simply for applying for the loan. And I haven't even mentioned the water and council rates that you'll probably have to pay up-front... boy oh boy, buying a house is an expensive exercise! But it can be worth it.

13 Buying the property

By the end of this chapter, you'll:

- know what type of property investing you'd like to do
- have made plans to start saving for the deposit.

Buying at auction

If you find yourself buying during a time when the market is really active, you'll find that nearly every property you look at will be listed to be sold at auction rather than by private treaty.

If you've never bought at an auction before, be prepared for it to be rather intimidating and stressful. Don't worry — as long as you stick to a few rules you'll be fine. I recommend you go to a few auctions beforehand, too, so that you get a feel for what happens and how fast auctions proceed. This will also help you suss out the various strategies people use when bidding: standing at the front or back and bidding early or late are some of the most common.

> **Money terms**
>
> **Private treaty**—The sale of a property, usually through a real estate agent, by negotiation.
>
> **Auction**—A public sale in which the price is determined by bidding, and the property is sold to the highest bidder.

As mentioned earlier, you'll need to have your loan pre-approved before you head down and pick up your bidder's card. It's also wise to have had the building inspection done so you won't be in for any surprises—because if you do win, you can't make the offer conditional on an inspection or a loan approval. The winning bidder is legally obligated to purchase the property then and there, no cooling-off period, no way out.

The first rule that you absolutely must stick to is never to bid higher than your spending limit. If the bank says you can only afford to spend $600 000 on a house, then don't bid a penny over $600 000. It's very easy to get caught up in the atmosphere of the auction and want to win, but you must resist. If you don't feel you can keep it together, consider getting a friend to do it or hiring a professional to bid on your behalf.

The second rule is to try not to be intimidated by pesky real estate agents whose job it is to get the highest possible amount for the seller. They'll try and persuade you to bid higher or go over your limit, and say things like, 'What's another $5000? Go on, you'll never miss it'. Don't listen to them: be strong!

There are three possible outcomes of bidding at auction:

- *You win.* If you're the highest bidder, then congratulations! Break out the champagne; you're a property owner! You'll also need to break out your bank cheque, because you'll have to pay the deposit there and then.
- *You lose.* If someone else wins the property, don't take it personally. It just means that you're destined to own another (and probably much better) property.
- *No-one wins.* If the property doesn't reach the reserve price (the lowest amount the seller is willing to accept), it'll be 'passed in'. If this happens, usually the real estate agent will ask the highest bidders to make another offer, which the owners may accept or may refuse if it's still not enough. If they refuse it, they may then start negotiating with the bidders to find some middle ground.

Buying privately

The other way to buy a property is by private treaty. This is when you can pull all your negotiating skills out of the hat and try to get the best deal possible.

The price that's listed for a property is usually just a guide, and it's rare that a place goes for exactly this amount. Negotiating is kind of like a dance: you make a move and the seller responds, back and forth until you meet somewhere in the middle.

If you've visited lots of similar properties in the area, you'll have a great idea of what the property is worth and whether the price being asked is reasonable. Sometimes you'll find a mega-bargain, in which case you might consider just offering the full asking price so you're accepted before the owner realises that the property is priced too low. Most of the time, however, sellers have an inflated idea of what their property is worth and list it at a much higher price than they'll get. This is generally the result of the real estate agent telling them they'll be able to get x amount of dollars for the property just to get the contract, when they know it's not worth that much. No wonder selling a house is just as stressful as buying one!

If you're going to negotiate on price, by all means offer less than they're asking, but make sure it's still reasonable. A method that seems popular (but that I don't necessarily agree with) is low-balling, where you offer substantially less than the property is worth. I think it's better to be fair and make an offer slightly below what you'd be prepared to pay, rather than risk offending the owner and agent. That way, they're more likely to play the negotiating game with you until you reach a figure that suits you both.

Property investing

Even if you've bought the property to live in yourself, you've purchased a major asset that is likely to increase in value. Therefore, you can still be considered a property investor.

Investing in property is one of most people's dreams, but it's a reality for very few. Did you know that the majority of the richest people in Australia (and probably the world) are property investors? It's true: just check out the next *BRW* Rich 200 list. Over half the people on it will be property investors; most of the rest will be business owners and only a small handful will be stock market investors. The reason for this, as we discussed earlier, is that you can gain leverage from property, since most of the cost is covered by a loan rather than your own money.

You may also remember that we mentioned there are three main ways to profit from property: selling for more than you paid, renovating and renting. Let's take a closer look now at some of the ins and outs of these three methods.

Selling for more than you paid

Probably the most popular way of making a profit in real estate is buying a property, living in it for a few years until it's increased in value, and then selling it. As long as you bought well in the beginning and you don't try to sell in a bust period, this is a tried and true way of making great gains.

Money terms

Boom period—When prices are high and people are making record profits.

Bust period—When prices are stagnant or even falling, and people are losing money.

Like most investments, property moves in cycles, from steady growth to booms and then busts. Nevertheless, over the long term, property generally increases in value — and as we saw in the last chapter, property in capital cities tends to double in value every seven or eight years or so.

Historically, except during a major depression, boom-and-bust cycles haven't lowered property prices more than a few percentage points. Really, the only way a property will significantly drop in price is if something is built right next to it or close to it that would cause people to want to leave — like a sewerage plant, a six-lane highway or something equally undesirable. If you've done your checks, you'll have found out if there were any plans in council for such things.

I don't believe there is a 'best' time to buy property, but you can certainly take advantage of the small fluctuations in property prices. When interest rates fall, property prices tend to rise; and when interest rates rise, property prices tend to fall a bit. So, if you're buying for a short-term gain, it could be beneficial to look at what interest rates are doing. If you're buying for the long term, however, it doesn't make much difference, and you'll probably end up paying about the same whether it's to the seller or the bank.

One thing that people believe makes a big difference to how much a property price rises over time is the area you buy in — they believe you *must* buy in the city to make any profit at all. However, it's possible to make a good profit in most areas if you choose well. Let's look at two properties over the last five years, one in a Sydney suburb and one in country Victoria, to see how much capital gain you'd have made if you'd just bought and lived in the properties for those five years and then sold at today's prices.

In a Sydney suburb

Around five years ago you could have got a rather nice three-bedroom, two-bathroom house for around $780 000. This was during a peak in Sydney property, and prices were at an all-time high. Over the next five years, growth was somewhat slower (and one year there was even a fall), but even taking that into account, your property would be worth $1 048 400 in 2007! That's a profit of $268 400 in just five short years — very nice indeed. This is how those years panned out:

- *2002* — purchased property for $780 000
- *2003* — 10 per cent median growth, property is valued at $858 000
- *2004* — 9 per cent median growth, property is valued at around $935 220
- *2005* — minus 2 per cent median growth, property decreases in value to around $916 515
- *2006* — 4 per cent median growth, property is valued around $953 176
- *2007* — 10 per cent median growth, and you sell at $1 048 400 (profit $268 400).

* Based on statistics of median house annual growth for Sydney Lower North Shore at <www.domain.com.au>

In country Victoria

Even though property prices are a lot lower in the country than in the city, over the past five years country prices have also increased dramatically. I imagine this is due to people being unable to afford to buy in the city and moving further out, thus increasing demand in these areas. For this example, I'll use an average single-storey, four-bedroom brick home with a double lock-up garage. Here are the figures:

- *2002*—purchased property for $83 000
- *2003*—20 per cent median growth, property is valued at $99 600
- *2004*—18 per cent median growth, property is valued at around $117 528
- *2005*—minus 6 per cent median growth, property decreases to around $124 579
- *2006*—11 per cent median growth, property is valued at around $138 283
- *2007*—9 per cent median growth, and you sell at $150 728 (profit $67 728 — that's nearly doubled in just five years).

* Based on statistics of median house annual growth for the Gippsland region at <www.domain.com.au>

Of course, this doesn't take into account how much interest you would have paid the bank during those five years, as opposed to the rent you might have paid. (You'll be paying one or the other unless you have very understanding parents and still live with them!) But this simple comparison does show you that no matter where you live, property investments can do very well using the 'buy, hold for a few years, then sell higher' method.

Flipping properties

Another way you can make money with the 'sell higher' method is to buy a house you feel is undervalued and resell it quite quickly to someone who's willing to pay more for it. Often this involves doing some quick, cheap renovations like a paint job and/or a garden spruce-up, so that the property is perceived to have a higher value. It sounds too simple, doesn't it? And you're probably wondering why anyone would want to pay more for a property with minor cosmetic changes. Still, this approach tends to work well in high-demand areas, particularly during a boom period when property prices can increase substantially in just a few months (or even weeks).

If you want to try this method of investing, it's important to do your homework. You don't want to be left holding a property you can't resell quickly, because the loan payments might negate any profit that you eventually make.

Renovating

The second method of investing also involves slapping a bit of paint and maybe a new deck on the property and then cashing in on the value you've added. Like flipping, this works well in boom periods; but it can also work at other times.

Most people want to walk into a property and have everything already done. Dealing with tradespeople to get a new kitchen, bathroom or deck is a hassle that most would rather avoid. So, if you're willing to do the work (or rather, hire professionals to do it), then renovation can be very lucrative. However, you need to stick to these rules:

- *Understand your market.* Know what unrenovated and renovated properties in your area are selling for, and work out if you can still make a good profit after you've paid for the renovation work.
- *Don't overcapitalise.* There are many things that simply don't add enough value to be worthwhile, like expensive tiles, swimming pools and unnecessary extensions.
- *Get quotes.* Don't go with the first tradesperson you talk with: get a few in and listen to their advice as well as checking what they will cost. Cheaper is not necessarily better, so choose wisely, and ask friends and relatives if they can recommend people.
- *Don't do the work yourself,* unless you're skilled in a particular area. It's usually not as simple as the television shows would have you believe — many a tradesperson makes a living from fixing botched-up home handywork.

If you're looking around for properties to renovate, try to start with places that need just a little bit of work before you move on to more substantial renovation jobs. That way, you can learn as you go. As well as painting and giving the place a good street appeal by tidying up the garden, the best ways to add value are fixing up the kitchen and bathrooms and repairing any problems.

Playing landlord

The last method of making money from property is where you get tenants and collect their rent as income. How much rent you receive usually determines whether the property is positively or negatively geared.

Money terms

Negative gearing—A property is negatively geared when the rent you receive doesn't cover all the expenses and payments for the home.

Positive gearing—A property is positively geared when the rent covers the loan payments and any expenses and gives you a small profit as well.

Most rental properties tend to be negatively geared, which can provide you with a tax break but still means that the rent doesn't cover all your mortgage payments and expenses. On the other hand, owning a positively geared property means that the rent covers the loan repayments and expenses and leaves you with some extra cash in your pocket as well. As you would imagine, positively geared properties can be difficult to find. If you're on the hunt for one, your best bet is somewhere two to three hours away from a big city: positively geared properties in city areas are very rare indeed.

Hiring a property manager

Once you've bought a property to rent, you need to decide whether you'll manage it personally or hire a real estate agency. Both options have good and bad points. It costs money to have somebody else do the managing, but do you really want to deal with tenants ringing you up to get the toilets fixed on a Sunday afternoon? Make sure that you take into account the time and effort it takes to manage the property yourself, how much it will cost you to pay someone else to do it and how involved you want to be in the process.

One of the benefits of hiring an agency to manage a property is that they'll be up to date on the residential tenancy laws and the rights of tenants and landlords. If you're not knowledgeable in this area of the legal system, it's probably worth your while leaving it to someone who is. A property manager will also be able to check out the tenants before they move in and make sure they're responsible people who have a history of paying their rent on time and keeping the premises clean and tidy. This is no guarantee that your tenants will behave, but it might help avoid the kind of tenants from hell that are regularly featured on *Today Tonight*.

Choose a real estate agency close to your property, so they don't have far to travel if they need to chase the tenants for rent, and so they're knowledgeable about the services in the area in case of plumbing or electrical emergencies. Also, make sure you have a good relationship with the agent you choose. They're working for you, and should have your interests at heart.

Commercial property

There's no rule that says that you can only buy residential property. In fact, owning commercial property and leasing it to business owners can be a great investment strategy. For one thing, these tenants usually want to make major improvements to your property to increase its value, so that they can attract more customers into their business. You can also get relatively long-term tenants, as businesses tend to stay in the same place for many years. Also, the net rental income generally tends to be higher for commercial properties than it is for homes.

When you're looking for commercial property, think about the types of things that will attract businesses. While a residential property might decrease in value if it's near a highway, a commercial property might be worth more.

Make sure you get a good accountant and property lawyer if you plan on investing in commercial property, because the contracts can be complex and you might also be up for GST in some cases.

Accounting

If you plan to do any sort of property investing (or any sort of investing at all, really), you absolutely need to get an accountant. An accountant will help you work out any tax concessions or claims that you might be eligible for on your property, and will advise you on whether it's in your best interests to get an Australian Business Number (ABN) to purchase your properties under.

Don't try and work all this out yourself: you'll just give yourself a headache. A good accountant will be able to save you much more than they charge in fees, anyway.

So, what kind of property investment should I choose?

You've decided that you want to invest in property. Now you want to know which of the three methods is right for you. The decision is ultimately up to you, as is every decision in your life. However, this book wouldn't be very helpful if it didn't give you some sort of plan to follow, would it? So here goes, my beginner's guide to property investing.

I think the very first property you buy should be one that you plan on living in. Many people say you'd be financially better off to rent while you own lots of investment properties (and this does make sense). But owning their own home makes most people feel secure, whether they intend to resell in the future or not. It's wonderful to know that you're free to do with it what you wish, too. And with the rental crisis in capital cities at the time I write this, buying your own home actually sounds easier than competing to rent somewhere!

If you'd rather travel the world for the next few years, of course, then buying a house to live in isn't going to be high on your agenda. For the rest of you, let's save that deposit!

How much you need for a deposit is going to vary, but to avoid lender's mortgage insurance you need around 20 per cent. If you're buying in country Victoria, that might mean around $30 000; if you're buying in Sydney's Lower North Shore, you could need nearly $200 000. The deposit amount will also depend on what type of property you're planning on buying. For example, units are generally less expensive than houses, and two bedrooms are usually cheaper than three bedrooms.

However, as I've said earlier, your first step should be to sit down and work out the repayments you can afford to pay. As a guide, I think around 30 per cent of your take-home pay is a good rate, but sometimes you could go as high as 50 per cent. I wouldn't recommend going any higher, even if the bank is willing to lend you more, because you'll find it difficult to meet the loan repayments.

Penny Saver's current take-home pay is $3907 per month, and she could probably afford to spend around $1700 to $1800 per month on repayments. That means at an interest rate of 6.75 per cent she could afford to borrow around $256 000. She'd also need a deposit of between around $26 000 (10 per cent) and $51 200 (20 per cent).

You may remember that Penny's dream is to live by the sea. She can't afford her luxury home right now (she's still saving for that), but she *can* afford a one- or two-bedroom apartment on Sydney's northern beaches. Granted, it probably won't be very big, but it will be hers and it will increase in value over time. And, of course, she'll be one step closer to her dream of living rich by the sea.

Homework

It's your turn. Write in the spaces below how much you can afford to spend on repayments (that's between 30 per cent and 50 per cent of your take-home pay). If you plan on buying with a partner, include his or her income as well.

I can afford to spend between .... and .... on repayments.

Next, look at the current home-loan interest rates and work out how much you can afford to borrow. (Hint: the online calculators at <www.realestate.com.au> or on any of the banks' websites can work this out for you.)

I can afford to borrow between .... and .... for a property.

I would also need between .... and .... for a deposit. (That's between 10 and 20 per cent of the property's value.)

It's time for the fun part now. Go out and visit the area you want to live in and see what you can afford. You can get a list of open-for-inspection properties from the paper or online at property websites such as <www.domain.com.au> or <www.realestate.com.au>. Look at around 20 or more places if you can, so that you get an idea of what's available in your price bracket — but don't worry too much if what fits into your budget doesn't fit in with your grand visions yet. Think of this as just a stepping-stone, just one step closer to your dream home. You see, the property's value will increase over time, and you'll have been paying off the loan, too, so in a few years you'll be ready to upgrade to something much closer to your dream home. If you love your first purchase, of course, you could choose to keep living there and buy investment properties instead. They'll also increase in value and help build a property portfolio for you.

But first, that deposit!

It's time to go back to saving and investing in term deposits, managed funds, and even the stock market if you want to. I personally wouldn't use any of the $10 000 you've stashed in managed funds after following the plan in the book so far. This money is there to provide for your future, and will also act as a buffer if the worst happens and you lose your job, get injured or need some money in an emergency. It's much easier to take emergency money out of an account than out of a home loan.

Yes, that means you'll be starting from scratch to save up the deposit, unless you already have extra money saved that you plan to use. But now that you're a savvy investor, it should take no time at all!

Buying your second property

After you've bought your first home (the one you're going to live in), you can make a decision about what sort of investment property you'd like to buy in the future. Maybe you'd like to try the other two methods, and buy both a fixer-upper to renovate and resell and a property that you rent out to tenants. There's certainly no law that says you can only own one type of property!

It's usually a good idea to wait a year or two after you've bought your own home to buy again, so that your home has time to increase in value and build up equity for you to use as a deposit on your next property. It makes it much easier if you don't have to save up for the deposit all over again!

Whatever property investing method you choose, you'll have to do all the same checks on this new property that you did with your first home. Once you've got one or two properties under your belt, the process becomes easier and easier because you can use the equity in your properties to finance the deposits for the new investments. The only thing that may stop you amassing a huge property portfolio is whether you can afford them all — which can be a problem if they're negatively geared. For this reason, buying a mix of rental and renovation properties is usually a good idea. Pretty soon you'll have lots of properties and be on your way to becoming a property expert!

STEP 5
Keeping your money safe

By now you should be well on your way to becoming rich. Your dreams will have started to come true and you'll have become much smarter about your money.

The next thing to do is to keep all that lovely money safe. It's not enough to just get rich; the trick is making sure you stay rich! This chapter will outline different options that will help safeguard your family and your money, like insuring your home and its contents, and writing a will.

No-one can predict what will happen in the future, but everyone can take action to protect themselves from whatever life throws at them. And, of course, this will be easy now, as you're already great at making plans and following them through!

14 Insurance

By the end of this chapter, you'll:

- have a good basic understanding of the different types of insurance you might need to protect yourself and your belongings.

Insurance would have to rank as the number-one most boring financial topic, but, alas, it remains one of the most important. The failure to get proper insurance can sink your financial future faster than Britney Spears' career. Yep, you need insurance to cover the cost of replacing your stuff if it's stolen or damaged, and you also need some for yourself, in case you become disabled or even die. Cheery thought, huh? But before you resign yourself to talking to an insurance salesperson, I'd better word you up about the different types of cover.

Home and contents insurance

If you own your own home, you almost certainly have home insurance already—the banks won't usually lend you the money to buy a place if you don't insure it. But do you know what you're covered for? It's a scary fact that around 80 per cent of houses in Australia aren't fully covered by home insurance, and most people don't know it until there's a disaster.

I don't want you to ever be in such a bad position, so the homework assignment for this chapter is to find out what your policy covers and increase your cover if you need to. That way, if the universe does decide a tree would look great sticking through your roof, your insurance company will sort it out quick-smart.

What to look for in your home/building insurance policy

Your home insurance policy covers the actual physical house itself, usually along with fixtures and fittings such as carpets, window locks and ceiling fans. It generally also comes with personal protection and liability insurance for any accidents that happen on your property, but doesn't cover any furniture or belongings in the house—that's what contents insurance is for.

Most policies will cover you for the basic disasters such as storm damage, fire and impact from a fallen tree, but policies vary from provider to provider. It's unlikely your home will be covered for a terrorist attack or damage relating to riots. Think those disasters are unlikely? I certainly hope you're right, but people in city areas should at least consider the possibility.

There's a lot of variation in what natural disasters are covered. Because of global warming, we live in an era where natural disasters are increasingly common. Things like floods, cyclones and drought can all affect buildings and homes, and you'll need to check your policy to find out exactly what your insurer covers. You may need additional cover if you live in an area where any of those natural disasters are likely.

Pet damage is another variable, with many policies only paying out for damage done from animals you don't own or have living with you. So if your own dog smashes your sliding glass door, you might be paying for it out of your own pocket!

Check whether the policy provides for temporary accommodation if the damage means that you can't live at home. This is important, because even if your house is unliveable, you'll still be paying the mortgage. You don't want to have to pay both the home loan *and* rent somewhere while you wait for your house to be repaired.

Lastly and most obviously, see if your policy covers the *entire* cost of repairs or rebuilding: don't get stuck with a policy that doesn't allow for yearly increases in home-construction costs. You want your policy to be for 'complete' or 'guaranteed' replacement cover, so you don't have to worry about spending over a specific sum.

Personal liability coverage

While most standard home/building policies cover you for legal liability arising from accidents around your home, it's a good idea to check how much you're covered for. Society is getting increasingly litigious, and you need to protect yourself. Ideally, your policy should cover you for at least

$1 000 000, so that in the event of a lawsuit all legal costs and associated damages (if you lose) will be paid. Some policies cover you for up to $10 000 000, but $1 000 000 should be adequate—check with your solicitor.

What to look for in your contents insurance policy

Contents insurance covers you for any damage or loss to your personal possessions. If you love your stuff and would hate to see anything get damaged or stolen, it's important to take out contents insurance so you can be sure you'll be able to re-purchase things after a burglary or fire. Even if you dislike most of your stuff, think about it: could you afford to replace it all at once if there was a fire? Even an old couch from Vinnies costs something!

As with your home/building policy, you want your contents insurance to cover the actual replacement costs—sometimes these policies are called 'new for old replacement'. This means that even if your TV is five years old, you'll be covered for a brand-new TV if it gets damaged or stolen. You might also want to check whether your contents policy pays out for things that are lost or stolen when they're outside of the home. If you took your laptop away on holiday with you and it got stolen, for example, would that be covered?

Try to be as generous as possible when you're estimating the value of your stuff—most people underestimate, and that means if the worst does happen you won't be able to afford to replace some things. It can be a good idea to make a list of everything you own or even to take photos of each room and store the photos somewhere else, somewhere safe. If you're computer savvy, there are plenty of great websites that will store photos and files for free so you can access them from anywhere.

If it's been a few years since you took out your policy, look at updating it, particularly if you've bought any major new items. And if you have things like collectibles, art or antiques that aren't covered by a standard policy, it's worth making sure you add them to your policy or get extra coverage.

Homework

This homework assignment won't be that much fun, but on the plus side, it should only take you an hour or so. I want you to go through your insurance policy documents, see what you're actually covered for and upgrade if you need to. It could save you potentially tens of thousands of dollars if there's a disaster—and being a savvy money girl, you owe it to your financial future to protect your home. If the fine print seems too confusing, a quick call to your provider should answer all your questions.

Landlord's insurance

If you own an investment property, it's a good idea to get insurance to cover any damage that your tenants do to your property, whether intentionally or not. It's a sad fact that most renters don't take the same care of your property that you would. Landlord's insurance covers you not only for any damage or vandalism, but also for loss of rent if you need to take the place off the market in order to fix it back up. It's definitely worth considering.

Like most insurance products, policies vary from insurer to insurer. You should look at the following:

- Make sure that it covers you for everything from holes punched in walls and doors to damage to carpet and floors. Damage can be accidental as well as malicious, so even if you trust the tenants, it's still worth getting full cover.
- Check that there's a legal liability clause covering you if anyone gets injured on the property.
- Make sure it covers you for loss of rental income due to the property being repaired or cleaned, or the tenants defaulting on the rent or doing a midnight runner and leaving you in the lurch.

Car insurance

To put it simply, if you own a car, you need insurance. No matter how good a driver you are, there's a good chance that sometime in your life you'll wind up in a fender-bender, and the other driver will sue you for damages to his car and injuries to himself or his passengers.

In Australia, you have two basic choices for car insurance, comprehensive and third party:

- *Third-party insurance* is a contract between you (the first party), your insurer (the second party) and the person you hit (the third party). It basically protects you against claims for damage that your car causes to another person's vehicle or property.
- *Comprehensive insurance*, on the other hand, provides cover for damage to your own vehicle as well as any damage you cause to others.

Compulsory third party (CTP) insurance covers vehicle owners and drivers for personal injury to any other party. It doesn't cover damage to property or vehicles, just anyone hurt in the accident. And as the name suggests, it's compulsory—you have to have this insurance to get your car registered in Australia.

So, which one do I need?

If you've registered your car, you already have CTP insurance, obviously. As for deciding between third party and comprehensive, it really depends on how much your current car is worth and if you could afford to replace it if it were damaged or stolen. If you think your car isn't worth comprehensive insurance, third-party insurance is a must: you never know what the other car in the bingle will be worth or what else you might damage in an accident. Even a small bump to another car can cost thousands.

If you bought an old bomb for $2000, of course, I'd say it's probably not worth paying for comprehensive insurance.

I recommend you put the amount you would have paid into a high-interest savings account instead, so that if you do have an accident and your car is damaged, you can use that money to buy yourself a new car or repair the one you have.

If your car is valued at substantially more than $2000, you couldn't easily afford to replace it or you've bonded with it and can't stand the thought of the two of you being parted, then of course it's best to get comprehensive insurance.

Life insurance

Life insurance is a type of cover that pays out a lump sum to your estate if you die during the period of the policy. Basically, if your partner or children or anyone else relies on your income in order to pay the mortgage, education costs or day-to-day expenses such as electricity and food (or even your funeral expenses), you need life insurance.

If you're employed within Australia, chances are that you already have some form of life insurance cover bundled with the compulsory superannuation paid by your employer. If so, great, but I'd be inclined to check your policy and make sure the cover is adequate.

Even if you aren't the family breadwinner, it's still very important to consider life insurance. If you stay at home to look after the kids, for example, your partner would need to pay for child care if you were to die. Child care is expensive, even with the government rebates, but a good life insurance policy will mean your partner will be able to hire the necessary caregivers without worrying about the cost. I recommend looking into joint cover for yourself and your partner in this kind of situation.

Private health insurance

You're healthy, and the Medicare system is reasonably good, so why should you get private health insurance? Well, health insurance isn't just about getting sick these days: it can also cover things like gym memberships, sports equipment and even massages. Obviously, though, the biggest benefit of it is access to high-quality medical services when you need them, without a huge financial burden.

Private health insurance may also save you money on your tax. If you're single, earning over $50 000 (the limit is higher for couples or families) and don't have private health cover, the government will charge you the Medicare Levy Surcharge. It's an extra 1 per cent on top of your income tax. If you get cover, the government waives this fee. So essentially if you buy a policy that's cheaper than the 1 per cent surcharge, you not only get health insurance, you also save money on your taxes. How good is that?

Even if you aren't in the right income bracket for the full government rebate, still think about getting private health insurance, just for the peace of mind it gives. Your health should be a top priority — after all, when you're rich, you'll want to be well enough to enjoy it!

So what do I need?

It sounds like you need a lot of insurance, doesn't it? Let me quickly summarise what insurance I think you'll need:

- *Home/building insurance.* You definitely need this if you own a home. It will cover you for any damage to your house or property, as well as for anyone getting injured on your property.

- *Contents insurance.* This will mean you can replace your stuff if it's damaged or stolen, and is important for both homeowners and renters alike. You'll want to be able to replace your things easily and not have to dip into your savings.

- *Landlord's insurance.* If you own an investment property that's leased out, you should definitely consider landlord's insurance. It protects you against things that normal building insurance doesn't, such as vandalism and loss of rent due to damage. Even if you trust your tenants, accidents do happen, and it's best to be covered.

- *Car insurance.* I'd get third-party insurance if your car is worth $2000 or less, and save what you would have paid for full cover in a high-interest savings account, so that if you do need to replace your car, you've got the money. If your car is worth more than you can afford to replace, get comprehensive cover.

- *Life insurance.* If you have dependants, you'd be wise to get life insurance. Check to see if your current work superannuation policy covers you for life insurance, and if so, whether it's $1 000 000 or more. Once you don't have dependants (for example, after the kids turn 18), you probably don't need cover anymore, so just get insurance for the period you'll need it.

- *Private health insurance.* I personally think everyone should have private health insurance, no matter how much they earn. Your health should be a top priority. I don't think you should accept anything less than the best services and doctors if you need them.

15 Wills and trusts

By the end of this chapter, you'll:

- understand the difference between a will and a trust
- have a will
- know what a power of attorney is and have thought about setting one up.

Life sometimes sucks. No matter how much planning you do, tragedy can still strike, and if it does, it's important to have the proper documents in place, so that your family isn't put under any extra stress. This isn't something a lot of people want to hear or talk about, but unfortunately it's a reality that needs to be considered. Wills, trusts and powers of attorney ensure that your affairs will be handled exactly the way that you'd wish them to be if you die, become gravely ill or are incapacitated.

Not too long ago, a member of my family ended up in intensive care in a coma after a motorcycle accident. He had been in the process of buying a house; in fact, he had paid the deposit and was waiting for the settlement in a few weeks' time. And while he had a will, he had no legal documentation to cover this situation, where he was still alive but unable to make decisions himself. He was legally bound to purchase the house, as he had signed the contract, but it was the family that had to try and sort it out while he lay in the hospital.

Most people don't consider that they might need any documents other than a will, but then, most people don't even bother about getting a will until they've accumulated a lot of assets! In fact, if you don't have much money, it's even more important to have your affairs in order. If you die without a will, the government will decide who gets the little money you have.

So, the two must-have documents for everyone are:

- a will
- a power of attorney for financial and healthcare decisions, in case you are unable to make those decisions yourself.

Once you're rich, you'll also need a revocable living trust.

Getting a will

A will is a legally binding document that names the people (beneficiaries) you want to receive your property and belongings after your death. A will is the only way you can ensure that your assets will be distributed in the way you want after you die. It should pre-empt any disputes among your family over who gets what. It can also name who will become the legal guardian of your children (or even your pets) if you and your partner die at the same time.

If you don't have a will, dealing with your belongings will be a complicated and often time-consuming process, and may be expensive and worrying for your family. Also, there's uually a set formula that the law uses to distribute your assets, and this may not be what you wanted—though contrary to popular belief, the government *won't* take all your money if you don't have a will.

It's possible to make a will yourself using the kits sold at post offices and other outlets, but I highly recommend that you get a solicitor to draft one for you. It's usually quite inexpensive, and considering that a will is one of your most important legal documents, it's worth doing correctly. If the will isn't deemed 'valid' because it was unclear or not properly drawn up, then the court will not grant probate (that is, confirm that the will is valid), and your property could be disposed of as if the will didn't exist.

Generally in a will you name at least one executor, who'll handle your affairs after you die. This could be your spouse, a relative or friend, or even your solicitor, and the person or people will be responsible for paying any taxes, debts or expenses left from your estate and then distributing the remainder to your beneficiaries.

Once you've made a will, keep it in a safe place, accessible to the executor. Usually, the solicitor who drew up the will can hold it on your behalf, often at no charge. This is a good idea, since it means you can have a copy at home and leave the original with the solicitor.

Setting up an enduring power of attorney

An 'enduring power of attorney' is a document that appoints another person or people (your 'attorney') to act for you in relation to financial decisions and, if you're incapacitated, in relation to health and accommodation decisions. You can make the power of attorney as general or specific as you wish, and state *exactly* what the person is responsible for. Obviously, you need to appoint someone you trust, as once you've signed the document, he or she can legally act on your behalf. Consider choosing a family member or close friend who understands your personal and healthcare needs. If you have a lot of money or property, however, you might prefer to appoint a professional like an accountant or trustee company instead.

You can give your attorney immediate power or specify a time when the power will come into effect. If you don't specify a time, it's usually assumed that it starts immediately. However, you can still carry out your financial transactions and decide about personal matters yourself while you have the ability to.

If you do choose a specific time but lose your capacity to make decisions before that time, the enduring power of attorney will start as soon as the person is notified of your condition. In relation to personal matters, the power *only* begins if you become incapable of making decisions. It's best to get advice from your solicitor about the best time to allow power.

Despite what you hear in the media, it's rare for someone to abuse the position of attorney by spending your assets unwisely or choosing inappropriate healthcare. There are laws under the *Powers of Attorney Act 1998* that ensure that your attorney acts honestly and responsibly. The person is required to take into account all your views and wishes, along with the advice of doctors and healthcare providers, and must keep all records and accounts of dealings relating to financial transactions on your behalf. The attorney is not allowed to mix your finances with their own, nor give away your belongings unless you've allowed for this in your power of attorney documents.

If you get your document set up properly by a solicitor, you should be adequately protected. As with a will, you can DIY using forms available from some newsagencies, but I strongly suggest that you use your solicitor instead. The power of attorney is there for your benefit: to make sure that if you are ill, in a coma or something equally bad, your finances and health can still be taken care of as you'd wish.

How about a living trust?

A living trust is a trust set up to hold your assets while you are still alive; the assets then get distributed to your beneficiaries after your death. It sounds similar to a will, but it's different in a number of respects. Most obviously, it takes effect before your death.

After your death, your will travels through the legal system and has to detour through the probate court before your beneficiaries inherit your things. Not only can this be costly (especially if your will is complicated), it can also take months. Living trusts are designed to avoid the probate process and may even help save you on death taxes. Under a living trust, your assets can be available to your beneficiaries immediately, which might be important if they are relying on that money to pay for your funeral expenses.

If you don't have any significant assets, then you probably don't need a living trust: it really depends on how simple or complicated your estate is. But since you're reading this book, over the coming years you *will* be aiming to acquire significant assets like a property or share portfolio. It might be worth talking to your solicitor about it when you're ready to buy those assets.

A living trust can be expensive to set up, but it can do much more than a will. If you and your solicitor decide it's in your best interest to create one, just make sure that it's 'revocable'—meaning that once you set up the trust, you can change it as many times as you want, so that you remain in control at all times.

So that's it. I know wills and trusts aren't the most uplifting of topics, but it's important to make sure that if anything happens to you, your wishes will be carried out.

Conclusion

At the start of this book I wondered if I was really the right person to write it. I'm not really that different to the rest of you. While it's true that I have a good handle on my finances and know a bit or two about investing, I don't consider myself a financial expert. But then it hit me: I was the right person to write this book just *because* I'm like every other woman. I understand starting from nothing. I get what it takes to start investing when you're new to it and aren't sure what to do.

Putting your financial goals in place doesn't take a degree in financial planning, and it isn't just for 'the rich.' All it takes is a plan, some common sense and the realisation that you *can* have a rich life. Anyone can, as long as they know what to do.

So if you're wondering whether you can follow the steps I've outlined and become rich, the answer is 'YES!' Nothing I've written in this book is new—in fact, I'm sure you've heard it all before—but I've tried to present it in a way that you can relate to, so you'll take action, take charge and become rich beyond your wildest dreams.

You might be wondering at this point what happened to our friend Penny Saver. Did she make enough money to buy her dream house on the beach? Did she ever get rich? Well, let me just have a quick look in my crystal ball at Penny 10 years later:

- Over the 10 years, Penny was able to save up over $140 760, which she invested into her managed fund. Her fund averaged around 12 per cent per annum, and is now worth **$274 652.**
- As you know, Penny purchased a small property in the area she wanted to live in for $290 000. Today, due to inflation and capital gains, it's worth double that—around **$580 000**. She does, however, still owe about $210 000 to the bank on her mortgage.
- She invested $20 000 in the stock market, and bought both long-term and short-term shares. Those shares have increased in value and she currently has a portfolio worth around **$90 000.**
- Her total net worth is $274 652 + $580 000 + $90 000 – $210 000 (the mortgage) = **$734 652.**

Now, her goal was to save around $800 000 so that she could afford her dream home. Do you think the bank will lend her the extra $65 000 to take her to her goal? Of course they will! They'll be trying to offer her more than that!

You're probably thinking that Penny's dream home would cost more than $800 000 now, and that's true. But if you want to go all realistic on me, during the last 10 years Penny's income would have also increased substantially as she got payrises or new jobs with better salaries. I doubt very much that she'd have stayed in the same job with the same income for 10 years in the 'real' world! So, in fact, Penny most likely has a net worth of much more than $734 652.

Penny could be you. I've used the current average wage and started her with absolutely no savings. She became rich by following a simple step-by-step plan. And if she can do it, so can you!

We've reached the end of this book now. I've talked about everything I know that will help you on your journey to becoming rich, and you're probably well on your way: you would have at least set up your savings account, started saving and made a plan about what to do next. Action is vital. Reading this book isn't enough to make you rich on it's own: you need to take steps to make it happen. But even one small action a day is enough to build a solid financial future. Like I've said, it's what you do with the money that counts! With time and lots of lovely compound interest, even the smallest amount of cash can grow into something amazing.

It's time to say goodbye. I hope you've enjoyed reading this book, and good luck in creating that magical, rich and wealthy future you've dreamed of. You can do it!

Index